How to Succeed as an Elementary Teacher

MARJAN GLAVAC

Previously published as an eBook:
How to Make a Difference: Inspiring Students to do Their Best

© 2019 Marjan Glavac

Title: *How to Succeed as an Elementary Teacher*
Format: Paperback
This publication has been assigned: 978-0-9683310-9-5

Title: *How to Succeed as an Elementary Teacher*
Format: Electronic book
This publication has been assigned: 978-1-9991631-0-5

DISCLAIMER AND/OR LEGAL NOTICES:
The information presented herein represents the view of the author as of the date of publication. The author reserves the right to alter and update his opinion. This report is for informational purposes only. It is not intended to provide exact or precise advice. The contents reflect the author's views acquired through his experience and knowledge on the subject under discussion. The author and publisher disclaim any liability for personal or business loss caused by the use of or misuse of or inability to use any or all of the information contained in this report. This report is a guide only; as such, use the information wisely and at your own risk.

For free resources for getting a teaching job, becoming an effective teacher and making teaching fun, visit:

www.TheBusyEducator.com

Table of Contents

Foreword

By Jack Canfield

There are a number of values that bond all teachers. One of them is the desire of all teachers to make a difference in their students. Unfortunately, this is also often the source of great frustration to teachers! Teachers often ask whether they're really reaching their students, whether they are teaching them lessons they will use, that they are making a difference.

As a teacher, I've often asked myself those same questions.

I had no doubt that I made a difference when I first met Marjan Glavac in October 2005, during a workshop I was presenting in Anaheim, California. He came up to me with a copy of my first book, which I wrote back in 1976 with Harold C. Wells: *One Hundred Ways to Enhance Self-Concept in the Classroom: A Handbook for Teachers and Parents.* He told me that the book forever changed him as a teacher.

Marjan's book *How to Succeed as an Elementary Teacher* will do the same for you and your students. There are certain success principles for teachers that, if followed, will make a difference in you and your students. This book will show you how. It's an instructional guide for teachers with practical strategies, tips, and techniques that work. The ideas contained in *How to Succeed as an Elementary Teacher* can work for any teacher.

Marjan has spent almost three decades teaching students. He has earned many awards for his teaching excellence from his colleagues and has earned the respect of his students. Many of his students have come back and still remember the techniques that he first used. His students are living testimonials that the strategies work and are still working.

If you want success in your teaching and want to be remembered as making a difference in your students, read and follow the strategies in Marjan's book.

It's a great resource for all teachers. I highly recommend it.

Jack Canfield

Jack Canfield is an American author, motivational speaker, corporate trainer, and entrepreneur. He is the co-author of the *Chicken Soup for the Soul* series, which has more than 250 titles and 500 million copies in print in over 40 languages.

Introduction

I sat in the principal's office. I felt helpless, emotionally exhausted, and humiliated. The last thing I wanted to do was to go back to class and face my students. All I wanted to do was to quit. I had been teaching for three years. This was my second school. My career path wasn't going well.

I got into teaching to make a difference; I wasn't making any difference.

I couldn't quit. It was my first real job. I didn't want to disappoint my immigrant parents. I was the first person in both families to have gone to university.

And in six months' time, I was getting married to the love of my life. I needed the money. I needed the job.

The next year I was being transferred to a much tougher school, my third school in four years.

My new assignment had me teaching French as a Second Language to seven classes of twelve-year-old students every day.

I taught every student in the small village where I lived. Students and parents knew where my house was, where I shopped, what I did.

There was nowhere to hide.

One day, my principal told me that parents at the local curling rink were dragging my name through the mud. They ranted about all the things that were wrong with my class. He told me that if my bad decisions continued, it would be very hard for me to live in the village.

Confrontations with aggressive, unmotivated, and miserable students dominated my life.

My classroom management skills were horrible.

The bell dismissed my students; not me, the teacher.

As soon as the bell rang, students ran out of my classroom like an unruly mob. They ignored my feeble attempts to tell them what was for homework.

Instead of working on lesson plans, I spent time straightening all the desks and chairs back into rows.

After only three years of teaching, I wanted to leave again. I was burned out, stressed out, and emotionally exhausted.

I didn't want to ask for help. I didn't know where to turn. I didn't know what to do.

....

Ten years later, the entire school staff, student body, and many parents came to a school assembly. They saw me receive The Prime Minister's Award for Excellence in Teaching for mathematics, science, and technology.

It was my first major teaching award. I was to receive four more.

I had just written my first best-selling book.

I was being asked to speak at international teacher conferences.

After twenty-nine years of teaching, I retired on my own terms.

I can help you make a difference in the lives of your students.

This book will show you the strategies and shortcuts on how I inspired and changed students' lives.

Justin, the most difficult student I'd ever taught in twenty-nine years, wrote how I changed his life forever:

> "I was probably the most challenging student of Mr. Glavac's **"most challenging class of his career"**.
>
> Coming into his class in Grade Six, in a brand new school in a low income neighborhood, I carried a lot with me. Like a lot of the 30+ students in that crammed portable, I came from a **broken home, with a low income single mother** stressed from raising two kids and working as a laborer in a local factory that laid her off more than gave her work.
>
> I had already been introduced to **drugs and alcohol via the local dealers who happened to be my next**-door neighbors. In twelve years of living, I had seen enough violence in my house, my friends' houses, and in my neighborhood to turn any young, impressionable mind into a savage.
>
> Most teachers would have put in for a transfer within the first week, but Mr. G took our class on head-first.
>
> Kids coming to school every day dealing with the above mentioned, plus some of them I imagine were hungry, and had illnesses, didn't... no...couldn't be expected to have much of an appetite for learning.
>
> Mr. Glavac recognized this and somehow came to see that the way to make us learn was to distract us from what was going on around us. He needed to find something that would **get us so excited about doing it and what the end result could be, that we would forget what was going on around us**, even if it was just from 9:00 a.m. to 3:30 p.m.
>
> The way to do this was technology.
>
> Most, if not all of us, did not have a computer, and because the funding was so poor at our previous schools, barely anyone knew how to turn one on, let alone type essays and send them electronically over this thing called the World Wide Web.

Well, to put it frankly, it worked!

He did have a few challenges still, however. Violent acts of rage and disrupting outbursts from me and some of the students who followed my still-unfound leadership.

Teaching home row typing to the kids who suffered from ADD and ADHD must have been hard also.

When I look back, I can see how from month-to-month, we were becoming less and less interested in acting out in class, and more focused on our new-found task at hand: to research and type stories, put them together in an electronic newspaper, and send it to schools around the world.

WOW! Most of us had never left our neighborhood, and now were going to be communicating with other kids from New Zealand!

And it seemed to snowball from there.

Mr. G sent out the word of what we were doing, and all **of a sudden we were being interviewed by CFPL News (our local network)**, TVO, Global Television, The London Free Press, and The Toronto Star.

We were shown that no matter what was going on around us, if we put our minds to something, we could do whatever we wanted.

We only had Mr. Glavac for one year, but what he gave us will last a lifetime.

And through it all, no matter what I did in his class, Mr. G never gave up on me and that in turn, taught me to never give up on myself."

I promise that if you follow the strategies in this book, you will get more accomplished in your teaching than you do at your current level. And I promise you will have the satisfaction of changing and inspiring your students to become the best they can be.

Don't be the teacher that procrastinates, who misses out on this opportunity to be the educator students respect. Be the kind of teacher that gains the respect of your students, instills in them a love of learning, and turns them into passionate and eager learners. Be the kind of teacher that other staff members marvel at.

Teachers who struggle with defiant and unmotivated students have already experienced great success by implementing the tips and strategies in this practical how-to guide.

Teachers from around the world have not only improved their lives, but the lives of their students as well!

Because this book is written *by* a teacher *for* teachers, you'll find it full of easy-to-implement strategies, tips, and techniques that will solve a wide variety of problems experienced in your classroom!

Believe me, no matter how difficult your current situation is, I have found a solution that works. And regardless of your expertise level, with twenty-nine years behind me, my book is full of strategies that have something to offer all teachers.

Sound too good to be true? Check out what others are saying about this amazing resource:

"How to Succeed as an Elementary Teacher" saved my mind. I was at the point in my teaching career where I was having self-doubt whether I was making a difference in my students. Reading the book and using some of the useful suggestions reinforced my decision to become a teacher.
Thank you."

Marian Wood
Co-op Teacher
Batchewana First Nation
Sault Ste. Marie, Ontario, Canada

"I felt inspired and empowered by your eBook. Parts of it affirmed what I held true about kids and other parts empowered me to make change even with my kindergarteners."

Cheryl Romer
Kindergarten Teacher with twenty-seven years of experience
Australia

"Reading your book refreshes my idea that I am doing a good job as a teacher. I have incorporated some of the ideas into my classroom with great results. I have used your book to help me see each day as a new opportunity to help my students succeed."

Crystal Ott
Sixth Grade Teacher
Danville, Iowa, USA

"This is my first year teaching in a public school (fourth grade), and I was ready and willing to accept help wherever I could find it. I have not been disappointed."

Liz Luebke
Fourth Grade Teacher
El Paso, Texas, USA

I promise you won't have to put in years of struggling and making mistakes like I did to become the teacher that makes a difference in your students.

That's my goal for you.

To your teaching success,

Marjan Glavac
B.A., B.ED., M.A.

Chapter 1:

Building the Foundation

Know Thyself

"A life unexamined is a life not worth living."

Socrates

"People don't succeed by migrating to a 'hot' industry or by adopting a particular career-guiding mantra. They thrive by focusing on the question of who they really are — and connecting that to the work they truly love."

Po Bronson, "What Should I Do With My Life?"

A successful class doesn't magically appear out of thin air. Success in the classroom begins with the most important element in that classroom.

There is one element that will determine the success of each student. The one element that will determine a successful day, term, or school year is you!

You determine the success. You lead by example. You make the difference in each one of your students by your thoughts, words, and actions. Don't let anyone tell you differently. You are the deciding element in your classroom. You are the first stone in the foundation.

This quote from Dr. Haim Ginott says it all:

"I've come to a frightening conclusion that I am the decisive element in the classroom. It's my personal approach that creates the climate. It's my daily mood that makes the weather. As a teacher, I possess a tremendous power to make a child's life miserable or joyous. I can be a tool of torture or an instrument of inspiration. I can humiliate or heal. In all situations, it is my response that decides whether a crisis will be escalated or de-escalated and a child humanized or dehumanized." [1]

To achieve success in the classroom, you need to know yourself. You need to feel right in your own skin. You must show students who have never experienced success what it looks like. If students who have never experienced success are going to experience success, they must see success in you. You must exude success; be success to them.

Knowing yourself means to take a hard, close, and objective look at who you are. This can be a painful process, but it doesn't have to be if you're honest with yourself. To come face-to-face with your own weaknesses, limitations, fears, and doubts isn't easy.

Your strengths, hopes, dreams, and goals are the sparks that light the fire of desire in you to teach. When nothing seems to go right, they keep you from going into those dark depressing days. Every teacher has them at some point. You must overcome them, then bounce back determined to succeed.

If you don't come face to face with your own weaknesses, limitations, fears, and doubts, your students will. They will find out your triggers, your buttons, and your stress points. You have to find them first.

So, how do you really get to know yourself?

Here are some questions that will help:

- What do you personally like/dislike about yourself?
- What motivated you to become a teacher?
- What are your hobbies, interests, and talents?
- What do you like/dislike about children?
- What do you like to do when you are free to do what you want to do?
- What are your most memorable moments?
- What made them so memorable?

Interest Inventories

Here's an approach I've found that helped me discover my interests and talents. In high school, I took a general interest inventory. It showed I had a high interest in writing, because I loved to read so much. At the end of my university studies, I took the **Strong Interest Inventory® Career Assessment.** This is a vocational interest assessment tool. Not surprisingly, English teacher was in the top three, right below lawyer and reporter. I also learned which subjects and careers least interested me. At the time, I didn't give the revelations much thought; but after teaching for many years, those weaknesses showed up in the classroom.

Interest inventories can confirm what you may already suspect! Knowing what I'm weak in has helped me a great deal. I've strengthened my skills by taking extra courses, asking colleagues for help, and asking my own students for ideas.

Discovering your weaknesses yourself is a lot easier than finding them out from your students. Or during a job evaluation.

Other personality profiles I have used and recommend are **The DiSC Personal Profile System®** and the **Myers-Briggs Type Indicator®.**

Both these personality profiles can show you:

- The type of person you are
- Your potential contributions to the organization
- Your preferred work environment
- Your leadership style
- Potential pitfalls
- What you're good at
- What you may not be good at
- What motivates you
- How to be more effective

This is useful information! Armed with all this information, the next step is to find out how people perceive you.

(I thought I knew my twenty-something son, until he showed me the results from his Myers-Briggs Type Indicator. I was surprised by what I didn't know about him. Now I better understand why he does things the way he does!)

Getting To Know Who You Are

Teachers wear many hats, play many roles, and present many different faces. The "you" your students see is different from the "you" your colleagues, administrators, or your family sees. When you first walk into your school, what masks do you wear? Are you usually in a happy and buoyant mood? Do you smile and walk with confidence? Is your back straight, chin up, and is there a bounce in your step? Or do you look like something the cat dragged in the night before? Are you grumpy, shoulders slumped as you drag yourself to class? Do your colleagues view you as a positive person? Or do you drag others down by complaining rather than offering solutions?

Are you truthful? Are you punctual? Are you polite? Do you listen with an open mind?

Do you under promise and over-deliver?

Are you flexible?

How do you react to parents who appear unannounced outside your class? Do you extend your hand and welcome them? Or are you curt and short? How do you respond, especially if they have been unsupportive and critical of you?

What would students most often say about you? What traits would they list? Why not ask them? Ask students to write down three things they like and dislike about what you do. The results may surprise you, especially if you already think you know yourself.

While they may reinforce what you already know, they may also show you what you need to improve and communicate better to your students.

Now, how do you want others to perceive you? Think back to all those teachers you had. What did you like most about them? What did you dislike? Which teachers motivated and inspired you to learn? What did they do to get the best out of you?

Which teachers did you dislike? Why? What did they do to make you feel that way? And what about your acquaintances and friends? What are the traits that you like or dislike in them? Why did they become your friend?

Think about your partner. When you first met, what attracted you to them? What qualities does your partner add to your personality, or bring to your life? Think about your other family members, your relatives, and the new people you meet. What stands out in each of them? What about them appeals to you?

In view of all this information, how do you want others to perceive you? How do you want your students in class to see you? And what about their parents, your colleagues and administrators? How much of the real you do you want them to see? Do you want your students to see you happy, sad, angry, or thrilled? How comfortable are you sharing these emotions?

In one of my schools where I taught for five years, my staff and students came up with this list during a recognition assembly (it's sometimes surprising to see how others perceive you!):

TOP TEN LIST OF REASONS TO ADMIRE MR. GLAVAC

10. HIS WINTER TOQUE.
9. HE OWNS A TIE FOR EVERY OCCASION.
8. HIS COLLECTION OF SHOES FROM STUDENTS WHO BORROWED HIS MATERIALS AND DIDN'T RETURN THEM.
7. FRENCH BINGO ON FRIDAYS.
6. BONAVENTURE MEADOWS HOMEPAGE.
5. HIS EVER INTERESTING, NEVER ENDING STORIES.
4. HE SURFS THE NET.
3. HE IS THE WEBMASTER.
2. HE IS THE KING OF KARAOKE.
1. …

Now you have come face to face with your strengths and weaknesses. Now you know your limitations and expectations. Once you become comfortable with who you are and you feel you truly know yourself, playing to your strengths and the strengths of your students will become easier. It will also be easier to offset, improve, and help your students to do the same. Only when you can accept "you" will you be able to accept your students.

I found it easier to admit to my students that I can't sing, dance, draw, or do a lot of other things rather than pretending. It's actually liberating when you can finally admit to yourself and to others your weaknesses. Especially if you are a closet perfectionist.

Start going into your class with the attitude that every day, you will learn something from your students and they will learn something from you. Be yourself in front of them. Resolve to do your best every day. In doing so, you will be taking the first steps toward making a real difference in your classroom. As you do your best, you will inspire your students to do their best.

NEXT STEPS:

1. Review and answer the questions in the **Know Thyself** chapter.

2. Go to the *How to Succeed as an Elementary Teacher Workbook* (found here: http://thebusyeducator.com/succeednow) and answer the survey questions.

3. Take the **Strong Interest Inventory® Career Assessment**, the **Myers-Briggs Type Indicator®** Personality profile/interest inventory from: http://www.psychometrics.com/or the DiSC® profile from https://discprofile.com

4. Try **5 Free Personality Tests You Can Take in Minutes** http://www.rd.com/health/wellness/personality-test-free/

Know Your Students: Part 1

"Forewarned is Forearmed"

Gathering Information: Part 1

The number one activity you can do to promote positive behavior is getting to know your students. It will help you become an effective teacher, minimize behavioral challenges, and have a well-run class. It is the next step in building the foundation for your class.

There are many ways to do this.

Start by reviewing the existing student files. Here in Ontario, Canada, a student's file is the Ontario Student Record, or OSR. At the beginning of the school year, our administration requires us to fill out a review sheet on each of our students. The information is then reviewed by a specialist called a Learning Resource Teacher. We flag students with difficulties for extra help and resources.

After gathering the data, you will be better prepared to develop plans for the individual needs of students related to programs.[2]

Know Your Students Class Review Sheet

(5 students per sheet)

OSR Class Review		TEACHER GR.		DATE	

NAME					
PARENT/GUARDIAN					
CUSTODY					
PRESENT ADDRESS: PRESENT PHONE #					
DATE OF BIRTH (YR. MO. DAY)	__ __ __	__ __ __	__ __ __	__ __ __	__ __ __
AGE AS OF SEPT. 1	__yr__mo	__yr__mo	__yr__mo	__yr__mo	__yr__mo

RETAINED	YES/NO GRADE(S) _____	YES/NO GRADE(S) _____	YES/NO GRADE(S) _____	YES/NO GRADE(S) _____	YES/NO GRADE(S) _____
NUMBER OF SCHOOLS SINCE KINDERGARTEN					
ABSENT/LATES LAST YEAR	Absents _____ Lates _____	Absents _____ Lates _____	Absents _____ Lates _____	Absents _____ Lates _____	Absents _____ Lates _____
CIRCLE IEP ESL	IEP ESL	IEP ESL	IEP ESL	IEP ESL	IEP ESL
IEP EXCEPTIONALITY					
CIRCLE LAST EARLY ID	SocEm Phys Lang LringSk	SocEm Phys Lang LrningSk	SocEm Phys Lang LrningSk	SocEm Phys Lang LrningSk	SocEm Phys Lang LrningSk
TESTING RESULTS	Reading _____ Writing_____ Math_____	Reading _____ Writing_____ Math_____	Reading _____ Writing_____ Math_____	Reading _____ Writing_____ Math_____	Reading _____ Writing_____ Math_____
PREVIOUS RESOURCE SUPPORT? SP. ED?					
LATEST TEAM MTG. DATE					
SOC EMOTIONAL CONCERNS					
PHYS CONCERNS					
LANG. CONCERNS					
MATH CONCERNS					
VIOLENT INCIDENT REPORTS					
SUSPENSION LETTERS					
PSYCHOLOGICAL REPORT					
LEARNING AND BEHAVIOR REPORT					
AGENCY INVOLVEMENT					
VISION TESTING					
HEARING TESTING					
MEDICATION USED					
OCCUPATIONAL THERAPY					
SPEECH/LANGUAGE					
OTHER NOTES					

At the same time as I'm preparing the review sheet for the administration requirements, I'm also preparing my own personal review sheet. I zero in on the last year's report card. Here's the system I use for each student:

Personal Review Sheet

STUDENT NAME	
DATE OF BIRTH	
SCHOOLS ATTENDED	
LAST YEAR TEACHER	
DRA	
STANDARD TESTS	READING_____ WRITING_____ MATH_____
LAST YEAR REPORT CARD ENGLISH	READING_____ WRITING_____ ORAL_____
LAST YEAR REPORT CARD MATH	NUMBER SENSE AND NUMERATION_____ MEASUREMENT_____ GEOMETRY AND SPATIAL SENSE_____ PATTERNING AND ALGEGRA _____ DATA MANAGEMENT AND PROBABILITY_____
LAST YEAR REPORT CARD LEARNING SKILLS AND WORK HABITS	RESPONSIBILITY_____ INDEPENDENT WORK_____ INITIATIVE_____ ORGANIZATION_____ COLLABORATION_____ SELF-REGULATION_____
STRENGTHS/LIKES	
WEAKNESSES/DISLIKES	

I input the information into a spreadsheet or alphabetically into a 3-ring binder.

I then review the data to get a better idea of the student as a person in my class. I also focus on the STRENGTHS/LIKES/WEAKNESSES/DISLIKES section in the report card. Then I review and brainstorm how I can best help this student throughout the school year.

On the first day of school and during that first week, I gather more information on my students in other ways. For example, I will test students' spelling ability using the Morrison McCall Spelling Scale[3]. Then I will test students again once a term, using the initial test as a baseline.

To assess reading skill-level[4], I administer the McCall Crabbs Standard Test Lessons in Reading. I do three tests timed for three minutes the first day, and then another three the next day. Doing so gives me a baseline of students' reading and provides me some information for their reading groups. At the end of the year, I retest the first three tests (I also use the Developmental Reading Assessment or DRA[5] to evaluate reading about six to seven weeks into the first term). In math, I do a quick review of numeracy (adding, subtracting, multiplying, and dividing), using questions of increasing difficulty. Again, I retest at the end of the year to measure progress.

NEXT STEPS:

1. Seek out advice from your administration, resource people, and fellow teachers on formal tests they do with their students.

2. For reading and spelling tests, see:

   Gates-MacGinitie Reading Assessment
   http://www.nelson.com/assessment/classroom-GMRT.html

   The Developmental Reading Assessment (DRATM)

   McCall-Crabbs Standard Test Lessons in Reading
   https://www.pearsonassessments.com/store/usassessments/en/Store/
   Professional-Assessments/Academic-Learning/DRA-Developmental-
   Reading-Assessment-%7C-Third-Edition/p/100001913.html

   Morrison McCall Spelling Scale
   http://www.spalding.org/images/pdf/learningathome/spellingpretest.pdf

   Analysis of Spelling Errors (Kottmeyer)

Kottmeyer's is an informal assessment tool that provides information concerning the pattern of errors students may exhibit during spelling tests. It has excellent information concerning phonetic spelling errors. http://mrsztuczko.weebly.com/uploads/6/4/6/7/6467356/kottmeyer_diagnostic_spelling_test.pdf

Assessing to Find Instructional Level First Grade and up
https://www.readinga-z.com/assessments/benchmark-passages/

3. For fourth, fifth, sixth, seventh, and eighth grades math testing: http://www.hmhco.com/~/media/sites/home/education/global/pdf/placement/mathematics/k-12/saxon-math-homeschool/sms_plt_middlegrades.pdf?la=en

4. For fifth to eighth grade math testing: http://www.free-test-online.com/middle/5th_grade_math_problems.htm

5. A very useful article: 4-Part System for Getting to Know Your Students: https://www.cultofpedagogy.com/relationship-building/
Editable version of data chart: https://x78251kcpll2l2t9e46kf96a-wpengine.netdna-ssl.com/wp-content/uploads/2016/07/Deep-Data.png

Know Your Students: Part 2

"Forewarned is Forearmed"

Gathering Information: Part 2

Here are other ways of gathering information on the first day, first week, and first month of school.

One popular activity over the years has been my Autobiography Project. It starts with the Getting to Know Me survey:

GETTING TO KNOW ME

Answer the following questions the best you can (it's okay to leave blank any question you don't know).

1. My name is _____ .
2. Birthdate _____ .
3. Place of birth _____ .
4. Number of brothers and sisters and their names _____ _____ .
5. Five words that describe me _____ .
6. My favorite books/stories/computer games are _____ _____ .
7. My favorite movie(s) or TV show(s) are _____ _____ .
8. My favorite movie, singer(s), or TV star(s) are _____ _____ .
9. My favorite sports or hobbies are _____ .
10. My favorite food is _____ .
11. My favorite restaurant is _____ .
12. My favorite color is _____ .
13. My best friend is _____ .
14. My favorite animal is _____ .

15. Things I like to do with my friends _____
_____ .

16. My favorite activities when I'm alone are _____ .

17. The best reward anyone can give me is _____ .

18. My hero is _____ .

19. My favorite school subjects are _____
_____ .

20. When I grow up I want to be _____
_____ .

21. One thing I would like to get better at school this year _____
_____ .

21. I can't stand _____ .

22. A question for my teacher is _____
_____ .

23. Shhhhhhhhhhhhhh!!! My greatest fears are _____
_____ .

I have three reasons for doing the survey. The first is the information I collect, I use to make personal connections with my students. The second is that I can use the information to improve connections with my students and the curriculum. The last reason is this information is the foundation to fill out the next activity, the Getting to Know Me Poster.

You should be using every opportunity to connect with your students.

Here's one example of how I use the information to connect with students.

One year I had three students (two girls and a boy) who loved football. I used this information with the students by using sports stories in my lessons. Especially football stories.

When we played football in our physical education classes, these students became group leaders. I incorporated football when we had extra recess time.

At the end of the year, they thanked me for the extra time to play football (I met one of the students fifteen years later. He told me he pursued football at the university level. He reminded me of his time playing football in my fifth-grade class.).

By knowing students' interests, you can make other connections. I give students books to read from my class library connected to their interests. In personal conversations, I mention articles, movies, or TV shows that interest them. It shows that I care about them. It builds positive connections between you and your students. You become an effective teacher.

A reproducible copy of the Getting to Know Me poster can be found in the *How to Succeed as an Elementary Teacher Workbook*.

GETTING TO KNOW ME

Answer the following questions the best you can.
(It's okay to leave blank any question you don't know.)

My name is

Birthdate

Place of birth

Number of brothers and sisters and their names

My favorite books/stories/ computer games are

5 words that describe me

My favorite movie or TV show

My favorite sports or hobbies

My favorite food is

My favorite movie or TV star

My best friend is

My favorite animal is

Things I like to do with my friends

My favorite activities when I'm alone are

The best reward anyone can give me is

My hero is

My favorite school subjects are

When I grow up I want to be

One thing I would like to get better at school this year

I can't stand

A question for my teacher is

The Getting to Know Me Poster is an activity done during the first week. I post these posters on the bulletin board for parents to see during Meet the Teacher Night (I have parents fill out the poster when they come into the class that night. It makes a great ice breaker. It was surprising one year for a parent to find out that he was his son's hero.). This also keeps parents busy while I am meeting other parents. It's not a night for interviews, but sometimes it feels that way!

Multiple Intelligences Survey

Although Learning Styles and Multiple Intelligences theory as proposed by Howard Gardner in 1983 has become controversial[6], I really enjoy doing this activity with my students. It's a fun way of finding your students strengths and weaknesses. Students also enjoy learning more about themselves through this easy-to-do activity.

Be prepared for some surprises. One year I had a student who loved getting up in the middle of class and wander to the front of the class while I was teaching. After viewing his Multiple Intelligences Survey, I noticed all of his answers were in only two categories: Bodily-Kinesthetic and Intrapersonal. When I later met the parents for a team meeting and received more information about him, they also noticed the same behavior at home. It helped me understand the student and helped me build a better program for him.

I explain to students Howard Gardner's Eight Intelligences[7] (see below). I then have them check the **Multiple Intelligences Survey** boxes and graph their results.

Gardner's Eight Intelligences:

- Verbal-linguistic intelligence refers to an individual's ability to analyze information and produce work that involves oral and written language, such as speeches, books, and emails.
- Logical-mathematical intelligence describes the ability to develop equations and proofs, make calculations, and solve abstract problems.
- Visual-spatial intelligence allows people to comprehend maps and other types of graphical information.

- Musical intelligence enables individuals to produce and make meaning of different types of sound.

- Naturalistic intelligence refers to the ability to identify and distinguish among different types of plants, animals, and weather formations found in the natural world.

- Bodily-kinesthetic intelligence entails using one's own body to create products or solve problems.

- Interpersonal intelligence reflects an ability to recognize and understand other people's moods, desires, motivations, and intentions.

- Intrapersonal intelligence refers to people's ability to recognize and assess those same characteristics within themselves.

Multiple Intelligences Survey BLM 1.4.1[8]

A reproducible copy of the Multiple Intelligences Survey can be found in the
How to Succeed as an Elementary Teacher Workbook
(found here: http://thebusyeducator.com/succeednow).

Name: _____

Instructions: Check off each statement that applies to you.

Verbal-Linguistic	*Logical-Mathematical*
☐ I enjoy talking on the telephone.	☐ Problem-Solving has always been an easy task for me.
☐ I enjoy keeping a journal and/or writing stories and articles.	☐ I love to identify, create, and sort things into categories or lists.
☐ I like to complete crossword puzzles and other word games.	☐ I can easily add, subtract, multiply, and divide numbers in my head.
☐ I like to go to the library and/or the bookstore to get new books.	☐ I enjoy brain-teasers and games that require logical thinking, such as mysteries.
☐ I would rather spend my personal time reading than watching television.	☐ My mind is always searching for patterns or an order to things that makes sense.
☐ I understand more by listening to someone read or the radio, rather than from watching television or movies.	☐ Ideas put into a graph or a chart are easier for me to follow.
☐ Whenever I see a sign or billboard, I have to take the time to read it.	☐ Checkers and Chess are two of my favorite board games.
☐ I am often told that I express my ideas and thoughts quite effectively.	☐ I am good at estimation.

Visual-Spatial

- ☐ I often find myself doodling during class activities or when I am on the phone.
- ☐ I love to draw and paint during my personal time.
- ☐ I have a good sense of direction.
- ☐ When I read, I can see the story happening in my head.
- ☐ I understand color combinations and which color work well together.
- ☐ Geometry is easier for me than other strands in math.
- ☐ I enjoy solving jigsaw, maze, and/or other visual puzzles.
- ☐ I enjoy creating cartoon strips.

Bodily-Kinesthetic

- ☐ I like to move, tap or fidget when sitting.
- ☐ I like to do things in class that I can get out of my seat to do.
- ☐ I am good at most sports.
- ☐ I like to use tools to make things.
- ☐ I am always curious about how many things work and sometimes take things apart to find out.
- ☐ I would rather show someone how to do something, than explain it in words.
- ☐ I live a healthy lifestyle.
- ☐ I participate in extreme sports such as snowboarding, kayaking, and/or mountain biking.

Musical-Rhythmic

- ☐ I often hum to myself while I am working or walking.
- ☐ I like to make up songs and/or tunes.
- ☐ I have music lessons outside of school and enjoy it.
- ☐ I know the tunes to many different songs.
- ☐ People often tell me that I have a pleasant singing voice.
- ☐ I often listen to music during my spare time.
- ☐ I work better when I listen to music.
- ☐ It is easy for me to follow the beat of music.

Naturalist

- ☐ I notice similarities and differences in trees, flowers, and other things in nature.
- ☐ I learn best by going on field trips.
- ☐ I like to bird watch.
- ☐ I am good at forecasting the weather.
- ☐ I can name different types of insects and animals.
- ☐ I love learning about the stars, planets, and the universe.
- ☐ I have a collection of rocks and/or shells.
- ☐ I care about the environment, so I am involved in conservation projects.

Interpersonal

- ☐ I enjoy talking to people.
- ☐ I think of myself as a leader, rather than as a follower, when I am with my friends.
- ☐ My friends often come to me for advice.
- ☐ I prefer team sports rather than individual sports.
- ☐ I would rather spend my spare time with my friends than be alone.
- ☐ I like to do group projects and activities in class.
- ☐ I enjoy teaching others.
- ☐ I usually talk over my personal problems with friends.

Intrapersonal

- ☐ I am often told that I am a quiet and/or shy person.
- ☐ I am curious and ask a lot of questions.
- ☐ I know my strengths and weaknesses.
- ☐ I have no problem sharing my feelings or opinion.
- ☐ I keep a personal journal or diary to record my thoughts.
- ☐ Some people say that I am strong willed and independent.
- ☐ I know what I want and try to get it.
- ☐ When I have a personal problem, I like to figure out how to solve it on my own.

Collect the sheets and tabulate the results on the Multiple Intelligences Class Profile Graph. This will give you a quick visual of the Multiple Intelligences in your class.

Again, be prepared for some surprises. One year a majority of my students were *Bodily-Kinesthetic*. We had great physical education and dance classes that year!

With students' permission, I post their results on the bulletin board. I do this so students get to know their classmates. I also post it in time for Meet the Teacher Night.

Multiple Intelligences Individual Student Profile Graph

A reproducible copy of the Multiple Intelligences Individual Student Profile Graph can be found in the *How to Succeed as an Elementary Teacher Workbook* (found here: http://thebusyeducator.com/succeednow).

Verbal-Linguistic	Logical-Mathematical	Visual-Spatial	Bodily-Kinesthetic	Musical-Rhythmic	Naturalist	Interpersonal	Intrapersonal

Multiple Intelligences Class Profile Graph

A reproducible copy of the Multiple Intelligences Class Profile Graph can be found in the *How to Succeed as an Elementary Teacher Workbook* (found here: http://thebusyeducator.com/succeednow).

Number of Students								
	Verbal-LinEuistic	Logical-Mathematical	Visual-Spatial	Bodily-Kinestlietie	Musical-RJivthmic	Naturalist	Interpersonal	Intrapersonal

One of the most valuable sources of information on students is their parents.

I give the handout Goals for the Year to each student. I tell them that this sheet is homework for your parents. I model how to fill out the sheet for their parents.

This handout is a great source of information. Who best to know students other than their parents? It's an activity meant to involve parents in their child's education. It's also an invitation for parents to become involved by asking if they have any talents or skills to share with the class.

A technique used by one of my colleagues is to send this handout by mail to students. He tells his students to look out for the mail and when it comes, they need to give it to their parents as their homework. Since getting personalized mail is so rare these days, this will have a huge impact.[9]

Some principals encourage contact by teachers before the new school year even begins.

GOALS FOR THE YEAR

STUDENT NAME: _____

Dear Parent(s) / Guardian(s),

As we begin the school year, I invite you to assist me in helping your child realize and achieve his/her personal and academic goals. Please complete the questionnaire below in as much detail as you can. You have valuable insights that will help me provide the best possible environment for learning. I encourage you to take some time to discuss this information with your child before completing.

1. What do you believe motivates your child to achieve his / her goals?
    _____
    _____
    _____

2. What activities does your child take part in at school? Outside of school?
    _____
    _____
    _____

3. What are some of your child's strengths?
    _____
    _____
    _____

4. How can I help your child meet his / her needs?
    _____
    _____
    _____

5. I would like to see my child improve in:
    _____
    _____
    _____

6. My child may need special attention / help in:
    _____
    _____
    _____

7. How would you rate your child's study habits? How would you rate your child's work habits? (1 being poor and 5 being excellent)

_____

_____

_____

8. I would like to see a school project / activity / excursion centered around:

_____

_____

_____

9. Please share any other information that you may feel I need to know about.

_____

_____

_____

10. Do you have any talents or skills that you feel you could share with the class? For example, are you an artist or a musician? Would you like to share your career path with the class?
    Please let me know; our class would love to have you share your expertise with us.

_____

_____

_____

11. Best time to phone you?

_____

_____

_____

12. Best telephone number to reach you?

_____

_____

_____

Parent Signature _____

Thank you,
Teacher Signature _____

NEXT STEPS:

1. Print out (and make any personal edits) to the Getting to Know Me handout, the Getting To Know Me Poster, the Multiple Intelligences Survey, the Multiple Intelligences Individual Student Profile Graph, and the Goals for the Year handout in the *How to Succeed as an Elementary Teacher Workbook* (found here: http://thebusyeducator.com/succeednow).

2. Prepare a 3-ring binder or a spreadsheet to store the information.

3. Review five students every day in the first weeks of school.

4. Update the information when necessary.

Building Rapport

"There can be no teaching without compliance. There can be no compliance without trust. There can be no trust without rapport."

Anonymous

"Everyone who remembers his [her] own educational experiences remembers teachers, not methods and techniques. The teacher is the kingpin of the educational situation. He [she] makes or breaks programs."

Sidney Hook

The next step in building your foundation is building rapport. To be an effective teacher, you need to build rapport with students, parents, and staff.

Building rapport can be summed up by Robert G. Lee's *The 10 Commandments of Human Relations* and from *A Short Course in Human Relations*[10]:

The 10 Commandments of Human Relations

(1) Speak to people. There is nothing as nice as a cheerful word of greeting.

(2) Smile at people. It takes seventy-two muscles to frown, only fourteen to smile.

(3) Call people by name. The sweetest music to anyone's ears is the sound of his or her name.

(4) Be friendly and helpful. If you would have friends, be friendly.

(5) Be cordial. Speak and act as if everything you do is a genuine pleasure.

(6) Be genuinely interested in people. You can like almost anybody if you try.

(7) Be generous with praise—cautious with criticism.

(8) Be considerate with the feelings of others. There are usually three sides to a controversy: yours, the other fellow's, and the right one.

(9) Be alert to give service. What counts most in life is what we do for others.

(10) Add to this a good sense of humor, a big dose of **patience**, and a dash of **humility**, and you will be rewarded many-fold.

A Short Course in Human Relations

The most important six words: "I admit I made a mistake,"
The most important five words: "You did a good job,"
The most important four words: "What is your opinion?"
The most important three words: "Would you please…"
The most important two words: "Thank you,"
The most important word: "We,"
The least important word: "I."

Author Unknown

Once you know a little bit about your students, you can start developing a rapport with your whole class. You can also start to develop a rapport with individual students, especially those who may need extra attention.

An effective activity to promote rapport is to make a birthday chart listing all your students' birthdays. It's a warm fuzzy feeling when students notice their birthdays on a chart on that very first day of school[11].

On that very first day of school, I use other activities to promote class bonding. One activity is a memory trick exercise to get to know each other's names.

Here's how it works. Students sit in a circle. Each student comes up with a rhyme or phrase for their name: Robert likes to play baseball, Jim likes to swim, Dana is a dancer, etc. Each student says their name and their phrase.

The next student in the circle says, "That's Jim who likes to swim. I'm Dana who's a dancer." By the time it's the last person's turn (which is usually me, the teacher), everyone will have heard every one's names repeated numerous times. It's a great way not only for students to learn each other's names, but for you, the teacher, to learn their names as well.

Once students know each other's names, we proceed to the next activity. The Making Friends Scavenger Hunt is an activity to get to know your class and students better.

This handout lists tasks such as "Find someone who is: new to our school; has visited three countries; is left handed; is the oldest in their family; has seen two oceans", and so forth.

A reproducible copy of the Making Friends Scavenger Hunt handout can be found in the *How to Succeed as an Elementary Teacher Workbook* (found here: http://thebusyeducator.com/succeednow).

Making New Friends

Name _____

Date _____

Find a classmate who fits each of these descriptions. Ask that person to sign on the line. Even if yon don't fill all the boxes, see how many different names you can get and how many new friends YOU can meet.

1. Is taller than you	20. Has freckles
2. Is left-handed	21. Has a birthday this month
3. Waits to school	22. Has traveled to two states
4. Has curly hair	23. Has long hair
5. Has no sisters or brothers	24. Was born in another country
6. Has initials that spell a word	25. Lives in an apartment
7. Was bom in your city	26. Wears glasses
8. Is new to your school	27. Takes music lessons
9. Went camping this summer	28. Can whistle
10. Is the oldest in the family	29. Just moved to a new home
11. Has an unusual pet	30. Has seen two oceans
12. Collects stamps	31. Is the youngest in the family
13. Has blue eyes	32. Has a smart phone
14. Was in your class last year	33. Has been a hospital patient
15. Is on a sports team	34. Loves to read
16. Has been to Disney World	35. Has red hair
17. Has an eight letter name	36. Has a tooth missing
18. Collects coins	37. Has eaten a strange food
19. Has had a broken aim	38. Hasn't talked with you before

And finally—is really an expert about _____

There are a number of reasons I like to do this on the very first day of school: I get an instant snapshot of my class.

It gives me an opportunity the very first day to observe interactions among students. I learn about the personalities of students. I see who are the natural leaders and/or followers. I see students who have high self-esteem and those who lack confidence. I see students who tend to be loud and boisterous, and others who are shy and quiet. Students who have many friends, and students who have very few friends.

This activity also pinpoints students who may need extra help. Two ways I observe this is the number of times they come up to ask me for the answers to the questions on their sheet, and how long it takes them to complete the answers.

The scavenger hunt is the perfect opportunity to start another rapport activity. I take pictures and videotape students for my very own video time capsule of their progress (I'll be giving a description of the time capsule project later). I videotape two to five minutes of certain highlights several times during the school year. Doing so usually gives me between forty-five to sixty minutes of video, which I show to students on the very last day of school.[12]

The activity is also a way of making every student in your class special. It is a non-threatening activity. There are no right or wrong answers. There are no marks to earn. If an answer can't be found, I let students leave the space blank. The class discusses the answers. The sheets are then collected. They are not evaluated. Students know this.

Since we do the assignment in class, every student is able to do it. So, their first assignment is complete. They've achieved success on their very first assignment.

This activity is great at making connections and generating discussions. For example, question #2 deals with students who are left handed. We discuss all the challenges of a left-handed person in a right-handed world.[13] [14]

Questions #5, #10, and #31 always spark great discussions.[15] [16] I ask any student who has no sisters or brothers to tell the class what it's like. Then I ask all the oldest students in the family to stand. They relate to the class the advantages and disadvantages of being the oldest. I continue with the second-born, middle, youngest, and twins and triplets[17] (I avoid the subject of adopted students and foster children at this time. It is a sensitive topic to be discussing this early in your class without knowing your students and their parents.[18]).

Questions #4, 13, 20, and 35 get a lot of discussion from my students. It gives me an opportunity to talk about genes and genetics, and why students have the traits they have.[19]

Extensions

A team building extension you can use with the Making New Friends activity is the yarn toss.

Have students sit in a circle. Pick a topic to reflect on. For example, "I learned this about you" (a fact about a student).

The teacher models the procedure by taking one end of the yarn and tossing the ball to a student in the group. The teacher then states one fact learned about the student.

The student does the same (i.e. holds on to the end of the string and tosses the ball to another student and states one fact learned about the student). Continue until everyone has contributed and has become connected to a part of the web.

We are all connected

The significance of this connection is great. From a systems theory viewpoint, all individuals can and do influence one another greatly (Fullan, 1999; Senge, 2000). Though we cannot predict when and to what degree this influence will occur, we can predict it will occur. To demonstrate that we are connected and influencing one another in the classroom, I simply tug on the yarn and ask students if they feel the pull, which they do. I ask a few students to tug on the yarn. We can feel their tug as well. Then I ask students to gently tug on the yarn when they feel a tug. This time, when I tug, there are ripples of tugs throughout the circle. I explain that like this yarn, our words and actions influence one another greatly. Simply asking students to think about what they learned from each other today supports this point. It may seem rather obvious or even trivial, but viewing the classroom from this perspective has deep consequences.[20]

A good extension to this is the use of a community circle time. Students get to leave their desks to sit in a scheduled community circle on the carpet. I usually schedule this as first thing on Monday mornings and the last thing on Friday afternoons. Sometimes I will bring in a treat which all students share. Each student shares what he or she did on the weekend or will be doing on the weekend. Sometimes we use the community circle time during the week as a way to discuss certain topics. I have also used it to recognize students who have achieved a goal, or contributed to the class or school in a positive way. I find the community circle time to be a great opportunity to build class rapport and teamwork skills.

Building Rapport with Parents

In the last chapter, we started to build a rapport with parents through the Goals for the Year handout. We're going to follow up and reinforce our efforts by a simple yet effective tool. It's called the "Sunshine Call".

This is a phone call to give parents positive news. It is very effective, for two reasons: firstly, because parents of students who are often in trouble at school don't usually get these calls; secondly, because we tend to phone parents to give them bad news rather than good news.

One of the first things I do the very first day is to catch students doing something positive. It's not hard to find something positive in a very busy yet non-threatening day. When I find that positive "something", I make a Sunshine Call to their parents.

Early in the school year, most schools have a parent-teacher open house night; sometimes known as "Meet the 'Creature' Night". A week before this event is a good time to build rapport with parents. This can increase your parent participation. I make Sunshine Calls to parents reminding them about the event. I make sure to include something positive about their child. I then ask if the parent has any questions or concerns about the first days of school. I also ask if there is anything they would like me to know about their child. Often what they say comes as a surprise to me, so I thank them for sharing that information.

One year, I was teaching in a very small town. It was so small that I taught every twelve-year-old in the town. Consequently, I was teaching a number of my friends', neighbors', and my colleagues' children.

Early in the school year, I gave a Sunshine Call to one of my teacher friends. Although her son was a superb student, the first reaction I got was, "What's wrong? What did he do?" And this was from a friend that knew me and about a child that was a wonderful student!

Imagine the kind of reaction you'll get from a parent who gets a number of Sunshine Calls from you those first days and weeks of school. This is especially so if, in the past, they'd received nothing but bad news about the child.

Sunshine Calls are a great way of building rapport early in the year with parents, and with your high needs students. Building rapport early encourages students to work with you even when things aren't going well. Moreover, you likely will get much-needed support from parents when you need it.

If you can get a parent on your side early, behavioral problems are easier to solve (one thing I've learned is to make the first Sunshine Calls to parents of students who may not have had good relations with the school. This early positive outreach will make a difference in your future interactions with difficult parents and students.).

This approach pays dividends in other ways. Parents will reach out to you.

It is very common in Ontarian schools for parents to remove students for vacations during the school year. In my early years, I would cringe when a student said that they were going to Florida, the Middle East, or India for a family vacation. To me, nothing was more important than being in school. But if you value family, this travel experience[21] reinforces those values. Students aren't entirely free from school. Here's an example of one the letters I received about a family vacation:

Mr. Glavac,

Hello. Just wanted to let you know that I will be taking Jill to Florida (6 days of Disney!) So, she will be leaving at lunch-time on Thursday (19th) and will return to school on Monday, March 1st. I will also call the office. It should be educational as well as fun, but very busy. If there is any work you would like her to take along, please give it to her by Wednesday.

Thanks

Dear Gloria,

Thank you for your note re: wonderful trip to Florida.

Since a great experience like this doesn't happen too often, I'd like Jill to do the following:

1. Keep a daily journal of each day's activities. Be sure to record the weather, major cities, different foods you eat, and the major highlights of your day.
2. Collect a sampling of tourist pamphlets from hotels you stayed at or tourist bureaus.
3. Bring back two newspapers.
4. Be sure to buy an autograph book and get as many autographs of Disney characters as you can.
5. Make note of different accents, words, and expressions of people you meet.
6. Be prepared to tell our class all about your trip.

Have a safe and wonderful trip. Enjoy the time with your family.

M. Glavac

Building Rapport with Staff

My former principal, Stu Cunningham, introduced the "Pat on the Back" to our brand-new school and staff. You trace the outline of your hand on a piece of paper and then thank someone.

This very simple gesture is a powerful acknowledgement that you care about someone. Don't restrict it to staff. Extend to anyone—students, parents, community members.

One year I made a Pat on the Back to our school's music teacher for a concert she'd organized. She put the Pat on the Back on her bulletin board. Anyone who came into her classroom could see it.

Ten years later it was still on her bulletin board when I retired (it may still be there!). A simple yet powerful example of rapport.

A reproducible copy of the Pat on the Back can be found in the *How to Succeed as an Elementary Teacher Workbook* (found here:http://thebusyeducator.com/succeednow).

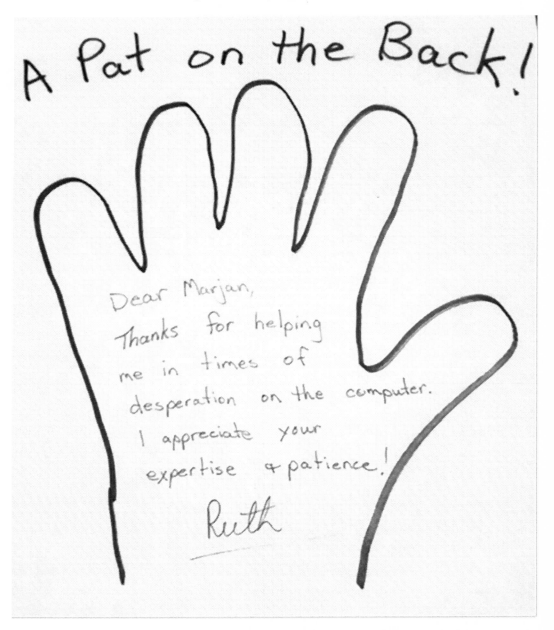

Here's a life lesson that former navy fighter and P.O.W. Captain Charlie Plumb learned that illustrates why we should care about everyone we meet.

Charles Plumb, a U.S. Naval Academy graduate, was a jet fighter pilot in Vietnam. After 75 combat missions, his plane was destroyed by a surface-to-air missile. Plumb ejected and parachuted into enemy hands.

He was captured and spent six years in a Communist prison. He survived that ordeal and now lectures about lessons learned from that experience.

Here is one of those lessons learned:

Recently, I was sitting in a restaurant in Kansas City. A man about two tables away kept looking at me. I didn't recognize him. A few minutes into our meal he stood up and walked over to my table, looked down at me, pointed his finger in my face and said, "You're Captain Plumb."

I looked up and I said, "Yes sir, I'm Captain Plumb."

He said, "You flew jet fighters in Vietnam. You were on the aircraft carrier *Kitty Hawk*. You were shot down. You parachuted into enemy hands and spent six years as a prisoner of war."

I said, "How in the world did you know all that?"

He replied, "Because I packed your parachute."

I was speechless. I staggered to my feet and held out a very grateful hand of thanks. This guy came up with just the proper words. He grabbed my hand, he pumped my arm and said, "I guess it worked."

"Yes sir, indeed it did", I said, "and I must tell you I've said a lot of prayers of thanks for your nimble fingers, but I never thought I'd have the opportunity to express my gratitude in person."

He said, "Were all the panels there?"

"Well sir, I must shoot straight with you," I said, "of the eighteen panels that were supposed to be in that parachute, I had fifteen good ones. Three were torn, but it wasn't your fault, it was mine. I jumped out of that jet fighter at a high rate of speed, close to the ground. That's what tore the panels in the chute. It wasn't the way you packed it."

"Let me ask you a question," I said, "do you keep track of all the parachutes you pack?"

"No," he responded, "it's enough gratification for me just to know that I've served."

I didn't get much sleep that night. I kept thinking about that man. I kept wondering what he might have looked like in a Navy uniform – a Dixie cup hat, a bib in the back and bell bottom trousers. I wondered how many times I might have passed him on board the *Kitty Hawk*. I wondered how many times I might have seen him and not even said "good morning", "how are you", or anything because, you see, I was a fighter pilot and he was just a sailor. How many hours did he spend on that long wooden table in the bowels of that ship weaving the shrouds and folding the silks of those chutes? I could have cared less…until one day my parachute came along and he packed it for me.

Think about this: How many times in life do you pass the people who help you out the most? The people who come out of the far corners of your life just when you need them the most and pack your parachutes for you? The people who go the extra mile, the people who don't look for the kudos or the accolades or the achievement medal, or even the bonus check—the folks who are just out there packing parachutes?

So here's what I want to challenge you to do. Look around your organization for the people who might not be the "Top Guns" of your organization, the loud and brazen leaders, but the ones who support the system that enables the Top Guns to fly. If something goes wrong it will be because they did their job that no one gets hurt or a customer doesn't go neglected.

This week, find five parachute packers in your organization and tell them how much you appreciate them and how important the things they do for the organization truly are. In the end, it might just be them who save your life or your business—or at least save the day.[22]

For more information on Charles Plumb, visit http://charlieplumb.com/

NEXT STEPS:

1. Print out (and make any personal edits) the Making New Friends sheet in the *How to Succeed as an Elementary Teacher Workbook* (found here: http://thebusyeducator.com/succeednow).

2. Make five Sunshine Calls to parents every day during the first week of school. Use the Sunshine Observation Form and the Sunshine Telephone Script found in the *How to Succeed as an Elementary Teacher Workbook*.

3. Be sure to log and document all parent calls. A Parent Contact Telephone Log can be found in the *How to Succeed as an Elementary Teacher Workbook*.

4. Add any new student information to your 3-ring binder or spreadsheet.

5. Get a ball of yarn or string for the Yarn Toss activity.

Building Rapport with Individual Students

"Kind words can be short and easy to speak
but their echoes are truly endless."

Mother Theresa

"People's behavior makes sense if you think about it
in terms of their goals, needs, and motives.

Thomas Mann

Building rapport with individual students in your class is one of the best ways to prevent inappropriate behaviors. Call it preventative maintenance for your classroom.

Building rapport by making a connection with students can start before you even enter the school or classroom. In some schools that I taught at, I was able to walk to school. Every student I passed, I would greet. My last school had a before and after school daycare program attached to it. Parents drop students off at 7:00 a.m., the kids start classes at 9:00 a.m., and then they go back to the daycare program after school ends. There they can stay till 5:00 p.m.

Doing so makes for a long day for some of these students. Some days I arrived early at school and had a chance to talk to these students and parents before school started. I sometimes dropped in on the students after school as well. This gave me a chance to see them in a setting other than the classroom. Doing so also gave me a chance to touch base with parents before major problems arose.

During my first year of teaching, I taught in a school where many students and parents didn't like the subject I was teaching. I taught French to every student in Grades 4, 5, and 6. It was a tough sell until one day, one of the students invited me to see him play hockey. He didn't think that I would show up at his hockey game but invited me anyway.

It was thrilling for him to see me when I showed up. What is more important is that some of my other students were playing on the same team or on the opposing team. They couldn't fail to notice that I was there watching them too. Yet the biggest surprise for me was the reaction of the boy's parents. They couldn't believe that a teacher would show up for their son's hockey game. Until then, no teacher had ever shown up for any hockey game. They saw me in a different light. Afterward, I could make a connection with them and I could see them in a different light, away from the problems of the classroom.

How to Build Parental Support

Soon parents and students viewed me differently. I was no longer a French teacher, but someone sincerely interested in the same things they were. When this happened, the tone of the classes I taught changed. Parents had always came up to me and complained to me about the problems their children had with French. But once I showed up to their children's hockey games, the support from parents grew. It made my first year of teaching a great experience.

Seize the moment to see one of your students play a sport or watch them perform in a play or band, or observe them in any other event outside of the classroom.

Especially do so if it is for a student that is giving you a lot of challenges. The small amount of time you put in may mean all the difference between having a frustrating or successful day with that student.

Hooking Disruptive Students with Sports

The one area of strength for many of my disruptive students is playing sports. Sports is not my area of strength. Since I needed to teach physical education classes, I got students to teach their favorite sport—basketball, soccer, football, etc., to the class (and to me). If you do this in a structured way, you can turn around some of these challenging students. Try to build on their natural leadership and athletic talents.

Three weeks before I introduced a sport in physical education class, I met with my chosen challenging student. We sat down and I asked him or her to plan out the lessons for the class. I gave the student any resources I had. I also told the student to talk to other staff members at the school who might've been coaches or who might've been athletes. In this way, other staff members got to see the disruptive student in another light based on the child's strengths and talents. I also introduced these students to some social skills. I taught them proper ways to introduce themselves, how to interview, and how to take notes. I stressed to them the importance of thanking others in person or through a written thank-you note. I would meet once or twice a week to touch base with the student and check progress. I also expanded on the social skills by having the student choose two or three others as helpers.

On the day of the lesson, I placed the chosen student in charge. He or she got a whistle and led the class as I would for a typical physical education class. This is a role reversal for both of us as I play the student while learning along with the others. Although the student is in charge of the teaching, I was of course still there in case there were any problems. And there usually were! The student, now teacher, often found out how difficult it was to manage and teach a class.

There were students who didn't want to follow the instructions. They would talk while "the teacher" was talking, and generally try to test or disrupt the lesson. That's when I would tell the "teacher" to blow the whistle.

In extreme cases, I told the student that the class has lost interest in the lesson. It was time to line up the students and go back to class.

Once students became confident and found their stride, the units usually went quite well. As I listened to the instructions like all the other students, I could see things from a different perspective. I saw them through the students' eyes. It proved to be a great experience for all the students, the "teacher", and me.

I've used this strategy with other subjects such as Dance with good results. Another benefit to this approach is the teaching of leadership skills. This approach bears fruit when your students move to the upper grades and come back to volunteer their skills and talents in your class.

Making a Difference One Student at a Time

As I was reviewing my students' files before school began, I noticed one student who had been in five different schools in five years. She had missed school for a total of 130 days over five years. Now she was going into my fifth grade class. There wasn't a single positive comment from any of her teachers. She even received a failing mark for physical education! There was nothing in her entire file that told me what her strengths were. Even more troubling, she had a history of defiance and being passive aggressive. She made a point to aggravate teachers in and out of class at every opportunity. Moreover, there was no record of support from home for any teacher meetings or phone calls.

Knowing this information, I had to become proactive. I needed to focus on how to solve the inevitable problems I would encounter with this student. In her case, I did many things. The first thing I did was change my perception of her. As soon as I met her, I shook her hand, smiled, and looked her in the eye. I said "Linda (this was not her real name), you are going to have a great year." I sat her at the back of the class beside a female student who was strong both academically and socially. I also put her in a group of students who could encourage her to do her best. Although Linda was a bit rough around the edges, she had a wonderful smile and was quite bright.

The first job I assigned her in class was as a point recorder. Every time the class did something positive that first day (i.e., followed routines, answered questions by raising their hands, minimizing transition times, etc.), I gave them a point, calling out Linda's name to record it. Every time something positive happened in the class, I associated her name with it. Linda was in charge of keeping a record of the points on the board, counting them, and assigning letters to every five points (once the letters spelled out the phrase "Let's Celebrate Now", the class would be rewarded with a cake).

Every time I noticed her do something positive, I commented on it. As soon as Linda filled out her interest sheet that first day, I learned of her interest in horses. I immediately found a book about horses for her to read at her level and gave it to her. On that first day of school as a positive reward, I sent her to the office. She had one-on-one time with the principal who rewarded her with a sticker and positive attention. He also connected her to another teacher in the school who shared her interest in horses. That teacher happened to have bought a horse ranch that summer. Before school started, I spoke to my principal about Linda's file and gave him a heads-up about her. I then asked him if I could send her down to see him as soon as she did something positive!

The second day of school, I made a Sunshine Call to her mother. I surprised her when I said that I was calling to say something positive about her daughter. I then told her that I sent her to the office…for something good! The mom admitted afterwards that she was scared to talk with me about Linda. I then made a point of inviting her to our Meet the Teacher Night.

So, how do you turn around a student like Linda? Baby steps. Small wins.

You can also try this effective approach to building rapport. As you go through your teaching day, try to catch students doing something positive. Compliment them on the things they do well. Keep track of all the negatives and positives you give out. Do you give out more positives then negatives? Which students are getting the positives and which the negatives? Do you notice a pattern? If so, how can you change that pattern for the better? As Mark Twain once said, "I can live for two months on a good compliment".

If we change our perception of students and have positive events to associate with them, wonderful changes can happen. This is true especially with students who are most often in trouble. We just need the determination to do so.

Meet Me at the Door

Another excellent way to build rapport and be proactive with students is to continue the first day routine with them throughout the year. Before students enter the classroom, meet them at the doorway. Speak to every student before they come into the class. Ask them about their weekend, how they're feeling, last night's homework, or the concert/game. Get them to tell you about sports scores, about their favorite athlete, singer, or movie star, and about any other interests they may have. If I have any students who are new to the country, I try to learn a couple of words in their language. They may be as simple as "Hello", "Thank you", or numbers up to ten. Either will connect these students to their new country and to you. You can also make sure that students prepare for class by having with them their textbooks, notebooks, pens, and pencils. At the door is also a good opportunity to "check their attitude".

Some of my students were on medication. If they seemed jittery, anxious, or upset, I asked them if they have taken their medication. If I saw that a student is too upset to come to class, I refused them entry. If they were having a hard time being polite, calm, and collected outside the classroom, not much is going to change when they're inside the classroom. Chances are they're going to disturb others while they're in the classroom! Instead, I asked that student to sit on the bench and relax. They could go to the office, the quiet room, or the resource room (either for their medication or for a time out if they need one). Doing so puts the responsibility on the student for their behavior and not on me, the teacher.

Some of my students needed a confidence boost. I did this by saying something along the lines of: "Rob, when I ask you a question in math this morning, the answer is 186. Can you remember that, Rob? 186? Have a great day."

I also used this time to ask students review questions about work I'd covered or about lessons I'd taught. If they got an answer wrong, they would go to the end of the line.

If they got a right answer, they entered the classroom and followed the procedures I'd taught them on the first day. They would go quietly to their seats and do the assignment written on the front board. This assignment was Bell Work. Bell Work is an assignment that doesn't need me in the class to teach. It usually involves simple math questions (seventy-five to one hundred-100 words) or short answers to story starters. It could also be anything else I needed to review and reinforce quickly with them.

Having students answer questions before they came into class gave me a great opportunity to review the teaching from the day before, as well as see firsthand if they had learned the material. If a majority of students had difficulty with this quick quiz, then I did a quick review lesson as soon they'd settled in the classroom.

Disruptive Thinking

One assignment I had for five years was the teaching of over two hundred seventh graders every day. The behavior of some of those students was very challenging. These students over the years built up many negative patterns in their behavior. As a result, it was very hard to teach them.

I used disruptive thinking to reach them. It worked like this:

I would ask my worst student to come in during recess. I would give him some money to go to the pop machine to buy two cans of pop.[23] When the student returned, I gave him one can of pop to drink and I drank the other one. I always mentioned something positive he had done that day or during the week. It's important to focus on the student's strengths, not weaknesses. And then we would just talk.

It was a very simple yet effective strategy. It disrupted his thinking of me as an authority figure. It created rapport between myself and the student. It gave the student a different view of his own self. When a relationship with your students involves something unexpected, the surprise breaks an otherwise too familiar routine.

I extended the strategy by using other motivators. I often took out a chess board and showed students the chess pieces. When I taught them the pieces, I would set up pawn games or simple checkmates[24]. Chess taught my students that there are immediate consequences to their actions. There is no one to blame but yourself in the playing of chess. Students quickly learned that to win at chess, they needed to know the chess rules, have a short and long-term plan, build a good foundation, set goals, and deal with unexpected results while remaining cool, calm, and collected. They also improved their concentration[25], visualization, and creativity skills[26].

Another motivator I used was to have lunch with a student and their friend at my desk. This was not done as a reward. It was done to get to know all students in the class. I provided the lunch of their choice. It proved to be another effective method of listening and talking to students and building rapport.

When You Need a Break

Sometimes you need a break from a student. Sometimes a student needs a break from you! There are times when there's that one challenging student who, for whatever reason, cannot exercise self-control. He or she may be constantly speaking out, teasing another student, or arguing endlessly with you. Instead of sending the student to the office or coming in at recess for a detention, there is another way without escalating a potential confrontation.

Make arrangements with a trusted colleague to give a break for one of your students in his or her class[27]. It's best if your colleague has a classroom far away from yours, but it's not necessary. Ask the colleague to take one of your students. The student can help the teacher with another student in class, or work on a given assignment.

When the time comes that you know a student needs a break, write a note to your teacher colleague with something like this: "Dan needs a break from the class".

This break is designed as a change for you, the class, and your student. I also reciprocated by taking my colleagues' difficult students when it was needed.

Some Qualities That Make Me Special

Have students give themselves a Pat on the Back with this activity:

Students brainstorm five qualities that make them special.

Students trace their hand on a blank piece of paper and print one word of their special qualities on each finger.

Students expand on each special quality underneath their hand.

Make sure to post on the bulletin board or in the hallway.

My Purpose

On a blank piece of paper, students write their purpose in one line and illustrate it. Post on the bulletin board or in the hallway.

Some qualities that make me special are ...

I am creative. I love art and I am very good at it.
I am friendly to one another. I am good at making friends.
I am good at helping people because when I need help they will help me.
I like track & field. Last year I got a bronz medal for high jump.
I love to bake. The best part is when we eat it

Cellphones in class

Humor and teacher creativity can go a long way to diffuse confrontations. Here are two examples (among many others) from a radio call in show on the Canadian Broadcasting Corporation radio network[28].

Patti Ellis, a high school teacher who retired after 29 years, had this to say about cellphones in the classroom:

"I found that the thing you had to do was not to make it teacher against the student. And I did it in some humorous ways…well, let's say the worst example that this was happening is Joe, who is skipping class. Again. Ok. I would say [to the class]:

'OK I need to borrow… is there any of Joe's friends here who want to, can lend me their cellphone? We need to make a call to get Joe to join us.'

So I would get any number of people.

I would ask, 'Do you have text or can I call? Oh, you can call.'

Everyone would be sitting and waiting. I'd phone and say, 'Hello Joe. This is Mrs. Ellis. Where are you?' And he would say, 'Oh, I'm in the cafeteria.'

'Oh, you know what? We miss you so much. You need to come to class. And you need to come really, really quickly to class.' I would say, 'I want you to listen to how much people want you to be here.' And everyone would clap. 'See, we want you to come.' And Joe would be laughing at the other end and you know he would come…And I would get Joe to come to class…"

"I had another kid who was chronic. Absolutely chronically missing class. And we had a Tim Horton's (a coffee and donut shop in Canada) across from our school until they moved, which was good. But anyway, I phoned him and asked, 'Where are you?'.

And he said, 'I'm at Tim Horton's.'

And I said, 'So you're not coming to class?'

'Well, no, I wasn't thinking about it.'

'Oh, but you know we need you and I'll tell you why we need you. Do you have any money in your pocket? Do you have enough money for two boxes of Timbits? (Ed. Note: Timbits are tiny donuts.) Big boxes.'

'Yes.'

I said, 'Okay, you get here with those Timbits in five minutes, I'll pay you for the Timbits and the class will be ever thankful.'

He came back with the Timbits and in five minutes, well it was really six but we didn't count, and when he arrived the class got their Timbits and yes, we lost a few minutes of learning and everybody had a good giggle.

At the end of class, I said 'I had to do this because I need to tell you that we need you and you need us and we need to be working together.' You know, I didn't have him skipping classes very often after that. He had felt kind of left out and he didn't feel that school was important and he still didn't feel that way, but he soon felt that he liked this teacher and he was going to come back for the teacher. And I didn't care what his reason was, as long as he came back."

Use a proactive, compassionate approach to prevent problems before they become bigger ones. You'll go a long way towards having a class and students receptive for learning.

NEXT STEPS:

1. Get to know your students as individuals. Find out their strengths, their interests, their goals. Create unique personalized activities to make them feel special.

2. Find a trusted colleague that will give you and your student a needed break.

Discipline: Rules, Procedures, and Routines

"If someone is going down the wrong road, he doesn't need motivation to speed him up. What he needs is education to turn him around."

Jim Rohn

"You can 'pay your dues now' up front, at the beginning of the year, or you can 'pay' later' — but you will 'pay'."

Fred Jones

What holds the foundation of your class from falling apart are your rules, procedures, and routines. They are the glue that holds the whole thing together. The best time to introduce them is on the very first day of school. The best way to introduce them is before students even enter their classroom.

Schools differ in their first day procedures. In some schools, students know who their teachers and classes are on the last day of the previous year. In other schools, students don't know which teacher they have until that very first day. Some schools have students assemble in the gym or outside according to class lists.

Whatever your school's method of delivering students to their class, what you do when you receive them is crucial. Your actions set the standard for the first day of school, right through the last day of school.

I would begin by going out to the playground. I read the names from my class list and had students line up in front of me. After reading all the names, I waited. I wanted their quiet attention by saying, "All eyes on me". I told them there is no talking while we walk to the class. Would some students talk while we went to class? Yes, unless you had already trained them to follow your instructions.

Here is your first opportunity to set the standard and reinforce that you mean what you say. If you hear the slightest peep out of your students, stop and have the entire class turn around and go back. Benjamin Franklin put it best: "An ounce of prevention is worth a pound of cure."

You must be willing to do this over and over again until students know that "you mean what you say and say what you mean".

Many times, I've found myself alone with my class on the playground that very first day repeating my original instructions. It gave me an opportunity to tell the students why we walk quietly through the hallway. We did so to not disturb other classes. Children are more willing to comply when they understand the reason to do something.

First Impressions

Once we got inside with no students talking, I had them line up outside our classroom door. This step may also take a few tries to get the class to quiet down. If the class is still noisy, you can use other options. You can wait until students are all quiet before moving. You can tell students that they will be practicing this during their recess or free time unless they're quiet. If just one or two students talk, I tried to let the group quiet them. If the one or two students persist, then I dealt with them. I cued them and directly told them what to do, or I had them practice during their recess or free time.

Before students entered their classroom that very first day, I'd already arranged the desks. I'd also determined where each student would sit. Your classroom arrangement depends on your subject, teaching style, and with what you feel comfortable. It also depends on the type of students you'll be getting. There are many approaches.

One teacher I knew would begin the year with no desks and no formal seating arrangement. The desks and classroom furniture were all piled in the middle of the classroom. He wanted to empower his students and give them ownership of the class. He did this by having them set up the class themselves. They decided on how to arrange the desks and the activity centers. He would also let them pick and choose their seats the very first day. It was a method that worked for him because he knew what he was comfortable with. He also knew the type of students he was getting. This is an example of how knowing yourself and knowing your students pays off.

Being Proactive

I preferred to set the standard myself. I avoided as many problem situations as I could by being as proactive as possible. Even before class began on that first day, I had already set up the desks in rows. Already I had the names of students printed on construction paper and taped to the front of their desks (this helps substitute teachers and teachers on rotary that come into my class to teach). I had also set up four extra seats with materials and assignments. These were for students who registered late and hadn't made it onto my list. Based on what I already knew about my students, I'd placed them according to where they could learn the best. I placed students who needed extra attention close to my desk. Assignments were already waiting for them on their desks. There was an agenda and instructions on the board. I had sharpened two pencils and placed them, along with an eraser, on their desks.

I greeted each student at the door by asking his or her name. I checked the correct pronunciation and confirmed that they were on the class list. Then, I shook the student's hand and told them to quickly and quietly take their seats and begin working on the assignment on their desk. I waited to see if each student complied. If the student is not quiet, I waited. Not until he or she settled at the desk did I go on to the next student. If a student does not comply and is talkative, I called the student back. I repeated my expectations in a calm, normal voice. In this way, all students entering the class have complied with many of my instructions. All this even before I'd introduced the rules of the class. I had also set the standard on how and what they are to do when they entered the class. This is the same procedure I followed every day. After the first day, instead of shaking their hand, I usually asked them a review question. This question is from a previously taught lesson, or a question related to one of their interests.

Once this routine is in place, students will be eager to answer a question. They will also remind you if you *don't* ask them a question! It's a great way to do some one-on-one instruction with a student. I checked their moods. I found out more about each student in a non-threatening manner. It's a great way to start their day.

Planting the Seeds

The first day is also a great opportunity to "plant a seed" with your high-needs students. At this point, I'd already identified some students who have had behavior and academic difficulties in the past. I usually extended my hand, looked them in the eye, said their name, and told them that they were going to have a great year. Your complimentary and positive attitude may be the first one the student has heard in a long, long time! You have given hope to the student that his/her year will be a great year.

I took attendance by looking at the empty desks and seeing their name tags, which I had taped on their desks. This took me less than a minute to do. I assigned a student to take the attendance down to the office.

Once students were all quietly working and completing their first assignment, I asked them to put their pencils down and have their "eyes on me". I then introduced myself, my expectations, and the rules of the class.

Some teachers prefer to have the students set up rules, through consensus or through voting. Other teachers prefer to set up the rules themselves and then discuss and teach them to the students.

There are merits in each approach. I have done both. Again, which you choose depends on how comfortable you feel.

Setting Class Rules, Teacher Directed

How many rules should there be? It's a good idea to have as few as possible. I limited the posted rules to six. The more rules you have, the more you need to enforce them. Take this opportunity to discuss what the routines and procedures are and why they are so important. We talked about their daily morning routine and why it's important to have a routine. Then we talked about the daily routines in class and why they are important.

These six rules were the basis of my discipline code. I also explained what discipline means. Students often think it's a punishment. I told them that discipline is doing what's right when no one is watching. When introducing the rules, I made sure my tone and body language was serious and business-like. I tried very hard not to make a joke or laugh when introducing these rules. If you want students to be serious about your rules, your actions should be congruent with your words. Lead by example.

Here are my Rules of the Class[29] [30]

1. Be in assigned seat and ready to work.
2. Bring all equipment and assignments.

3. Keep hands, feet, books, and objects to yourself.

4. Use appropriate language.

5. Follow teacher's instructions.

6. No food or gum in the classroom.

Procedures that will help you learn:

1. Listen carefully in class so you can follow directions the first time they're given.

2. Do not talk during inappropriate times.

3. Raise your hand, be quiet, and wait to be acknowledged when answering a question.

4. Respect the people, equipment, and furnishings of your classroom and school.

5. Line up and walk down the halls quietly when coming into the classroom and entering the school.

6. **Bring a positive attitude to class every day, use your time wisely, and give your best effort on everything you do.**

If You Choose To Break a Rule

First Time: Name in teacher's notepad. Verbal warning given.

Second Time: One check. Parent(s) contacted with a note in the planner.

Third Time: Two checks. Parent(s) are contacted. Detention and an action plan is completed by the student. The action plan is to be signed by the parent(s) and returned to Mr. Glavac.

Fourth Time: Three checks and parents called about the reoccurring problem.

Severe Disruptions: Student sent immediately to the office.

* A fresh start is given the next day.

Instead of a phone call to parents, you may want to have the student write, print, or dictate the information to the parent. In this way, the student also practices letter writing.

A reproducible copy of my Classroom Rules can be found in the
How to Succeed as an Elementary Teacher Workbook
(found here: http://thebusyeducator.com/succeednow).

Discipline Plan For, Mr. Glavac's Grade 5/6 Class Classroom Rules

Student Expectations:
1. Be in assigned seat and ready to work.
2. Bring all equipment and assignments.
3. Keep hands, feet, toots and objects to yourself.
4. Use appropriate language.
5. Follow teachers instructions.
6. No food or gum in the classroom.

Procedures that will help you learn:
1. Listen carefully in class so you can follow directions the first time they're given.
2. Do not talk during inappropriate times.
3. Raise your hand, be quiet, and wait to be acknowledged when answering a question.
4. Respect the people, equipment, and furnishings of your classroom and school.
5. Line up and walk down the halls quietly when coming into the classroom, and entering the school.
6. **Bring a positive attitude to class every day, and give your best effort on everything you do.**

If You Choose To Break A Rule

First Time: Name in teachers notepad. Verbal warning given.
Second Time: One check. Parent(s) contacted with a note in the planner.
Third Time: Two checks. Parent(s) are contacted. Detention and an action plan is completed by the student, The action plan is to be signed by the parent(s) and returned to Mr. Glavac.
Fourth Time: Three checks and parents called about the reoccurring problem.
Severe Disruptions: Student sent immediately to the office.
* A fresh start is given the next day.

Awards and Rewards

Daily:	Smiles	Weekly: Gotcha, Draw
	Praise	
	Positive notes home	Monthly: F A.T (Personal Activity Time)

* The best reward is die satisfaction of a job well done!

STUDENTS: I have read this classroom discipline plan and understand it. I will comply with it while in Mr. Glavac's class.

Signature _____
    Date _____

PARENTS: My child has discussed the classroom discipline plan with me (us). I/We understand it and will support it.

Signature _____
    Date _____

TEACHER: I will be fair and consistent in administering the discipline plan in my classroom.

Signature _____
    Date _____

* Please return this sheet immediately to Mr. Glavac. Thank you.

This also gave me the chance to tell them what a detention means. It comes from the French word *detendre*—a lessening of tension. It's a chance to cool down and consider how to make good decisions. When we're upset, emotions rule us instead of logic, making us say things that we later regret!

I also gave incentives for good behavior. These included positive notes and comments to students and parents, free time, extended recesses, no homework, extra reading time, extra physical education, game time, class parties, sending students to the office for a sticker, and a Pat on the Back.

As I mentioned, I don't smile when explaining the rules. I do smile and laugh and joke when I explain the rewards.

Restorative Approach to Conflict Resolution

My last school was a Tribes School. A few years before my retirement, my district started to implement a "Restorative Approach to Conflict Resolution".[31] The two approaches go hand in hand. I incorporated the Tribes' Four Agreements with my discipline plan.

Tribes Agreement poster posted beside class rules

Attentive listening: Involves paying close attention to one another's expression of ideas, opinions, and feelings; to check for understanding and letting others know they have been heard. All of these are teachable social skills and involve maintaining eye contact, withholding your own comments, paraphrasing key words to show you've been listening and using body language, listening with your ears, your eyes, and your heart

Appreciation/no put downs: Aims to develop a sense of self-esteem and self-worth through appreciation and recognition of each other's gifts and talents. As a community, we treat others kindly, state appreciations for all individuals and avoid negative remarks, name calling, or hateful gestures/behaviors.

Mutual respect: To ensure that cultural values, beliefs, and needs will be considered and honored. Students learn to respect individual skills, talents, and contributions. By using mutual respect, students are able to offer each other feedback that encourages growth.

The right to pass: Each person has the right to choose the extent to which she or he will share in a group activity. Choosing the right to pass means that the person prefers not to share personal information or feelings, or to actively participate in the group at a particular moment. Being a silent observer is still a form of participation and can lead to greater learning.

Traditional Approach vs. Restorative Approach to Conflict Resolution [32]

Traditional

focuses on the past and ranges from punitive to neglectful to permissive responses. Ask:

- What rules have been broken?
- Who did it?
- What consequence/punishment is deserved?

Restorative

looks at past incidents in the present, with a view to creating a better future for all involved, and focuses on working with each other to build and restore relationships. Ask:

- Who has been hurt?

- How have they been affected?
- All involved need to consider what should be done to make things right and, by doing so, restore relationships.

Restorative Approaches Value:

- Mutual respect.
- Character development.
- Acceptance of diversity.
- The belief that people have the capacity to change.
- The belief that given time, support and a chance to explain, problems can be resolved.
- An inclusive approach to problem solving where feelings, needs and views of all involved are considered.
- Building and maintaining respectful relationships.
- The creation of a safe inclusive culture of caring.

Whole School Practices for a Safe, Inclusive Culture of Caring		
ACTIONS **BUILDING** Tribes, Instructional Intelligence, Differentiated Instruction, Learning Cycles	**REPAIRING** Peer Mediation, Problem Solving Circles, Informal Conferencing, Restorative Questions, Gives voice to the harmed	**RESTORING** Formal Restorative Conferencing, Mediation
OUTCOMES Developing Character Through Social, Emotional, and Academic Learning **IMPROVE STUDENT LEARNING** Social and school engagement, build empathy, build and maintain relationships in school and community	Managing Difficulties and Disruptions **KEEPING STUDENTS IN CLASS** reduce office referrals, increased cooperation	Restoring Relationships **KEEP STUDENTS IN SCHOOL** reduce suspension and expulsion rates

Creating a Culture of Restorative Approaches

Questions for people who have been harmed

What have you been thinking about since this happened?

What has this been like for you and others?

What has been the worst part of all of this?

What do you think needs to happen to make things right?

How can we support you?

Questions for people who have caused harm

What happened?

What were you thinking at the time?

What have you thought about since?

Who has been affected by what you have done?

How have they been affected?

What do you need to do to make things right?

How can we support you?

Whichever system you choose for your class rules, procedures, routines, and discipline policy, be consistent in enforcing them. It is a key ingredient for being an effective teacher[33].

NEXT STEPS:

1. Before deciding on a discipline plan for your class, find out the school's discipline policy, problem solving model, and code of conduct.

2. Enquire from the administration or other teachers what the entry procedures are for the first day.

3. Decide on your desk arrangement and seating plan (refer to your notes on each student).

4. Decide on procedures for students' coats and backpacks, their entrance into the class, and expectations once they are in the class.

5. Read my handouts on Discipline: Rules, Procedures, and Routines in the *How to Succeed as an Elementary Teacher Workbook* (found here: http://thebusyeducator.com/succeednow).

6. Decide your classroom rules.

Goal Setting: A Tool of Success

"What you can do, or dream you can do, begin it;
boldness has genius, power, and magic in it."

Johann Wolfgang von Goethe

"Remember, little steps are easier than big steps,
so once you have your plan in place, don't think about the mountain.
Focus instead on the next plateau."

AppleOne https://www.appleone.ca/

What amazes me with my students is that time after time, year after year, a lot of them don't know how to achieve success. School should be a great place to teach children the methods to achieve success.

One concept that I introduced early in the year are very effective principles of goal setting. Some students in the early grades have heard about the importance of goals (they know the concept of scoring a goal in hockey or in soccer). By their high school years, virtually all students have heard about the need to set goals. Few students, however, are taught how to achieve their goals.

One day my principal walked into my class as I was teaching about goal setting. I had just asked my Grade Five class, "How can you eat an elephant?" After a long pause, I asked my principal and he answered, "One bite at a time!" After another long pause, my students started to get it. I told them that no matter how huge the goal may be, "a journey of a thousand miles begins with the first step".

It was at this point that I told students that everything is incremental or baby steps.[34] I gave them the example of me and my weight. I didn't put on twenty extra pounds all at once. Over the years, I'd exercised less and less, and ate a bit more and more, until I started to put on an extra pound (or two) a year. Over twenty years, those pounds added up! Since it took me twenty years to gain the extra weight, I was not going to lose it all at once.

How to Set Goals

Reaching most goals takes one step at a time. The most important thing is to get started. I made a conscious effort many years ago to get back into shape and exercise. I'm often too tired to exercise before and after school, so I started to exercise with my students by running and doing stretches with them during our physical education classes. I not only showed students how goal setting works in theory, but also in practice.

Early in the year, I distributed a goal-setting handout to the students. I make a transparency for the overhead or for the whiteboard. I also recite the poem "Mother to Son" by Langston Hughes[35]. Then I explain each point to the students.

A reproducible copy of the "Goal Setting: A Tool of Success" handout can be found in the *How to Succeed as an Elementary Teacher Workbook* (found here: http://thebusyeducator.com/succeednow).

Goal Setting A Tool of Success

Name _____

Date _____

GOAL
My goal is_____

STEPS
To reach my goal I **plan** to take these steps:

1. _____
2. _____
3. _____

HELPERS
These are the people who can help me:

1. _____
2. _____
3. _____

OBSTACLES
I must watch out for:

1. _____
2. _____
3. _____

TIMELINE

I plan to achieve this goal by:

_____

Reward

My reward for successfully achieving this goal will be:

_____

I first started this practical goal-setting exercise with my students fifteen years ago. My goal was to run five minutes non-stop by the end of the school year in June. That was no easy task. I tried all summer before school started to get into shape by running. Although I ran in high school and partly throughout university, I couldn't run more than one and a half minutes! For some time, I couldn't break that barrier. So, I went "public". I told my students my goal. I wrote it down. I then posted it for all to see. I wanted to show my students how to put a goal in place.

I am happy to write that before the year was over, I did achieve the goal of running five minutes without stopping. The next year, I doubled the goal to ten minutes. I showed those students how to achieve their goals while I modeled how to achieve mine. Again, I succeeded. Flushed with success and confidence, the following year I doubled the goal to twenty minutes. That was definitely a yearlong goal, which I succeeded in achieving. The following year I continued with the goal, increasing it to thirty minutes and then to sixty minutes. Both goals were also achieved.

Another goal I shared with students was to lose twenty pounds in six months. I surpassed it by losing twenty-two pounds in six months. I brought in twenty-two pounds of sugar and put it on my desk as a visual aid for my students. I told my students that this was how much weight I lost in six months. I then asked them, how many pounds did I lose per month, per week?

I told students that their goals don't need to be school goals. Over the years, their goals included doing more reading, to becoming a better soccer goalie, getting an advanced yellow belt in karate, earning more I Did It Awards, scoring a goal in hockey, and watching less T.V. Some students duplicated my goal of running.

Knowing these students' goals and what's important to them gives teachers a great opportunity to help students to connect them to success. This is an ideal way to engage students into goal setting.

If I knew that a student is looking for a babysitting job and I knew parents who are looking for a babysitter, I could connect them.

It was the same for students looking for jobs or places on the school team. If I knew someone who could help them, I would connect them. This approach also showed students the power of networking and getting to know other people.

I also posted student goals on the bulletin board for this very reason. Their peers (and parents and other teachers visiting the classroom) might also know of ways to help them achieve their goals.

Over the years students' goals have ranged from:

- Watch less T.V.
- To get better at spelling.
- Score a goal in hockey.
- Get better at timed math tests.
- To get a good mark on my report card.
- Learn how to play tennis.
- Get an advanced yellow belt in Karate.
- Make friends.
- To be a more fluent reader.
- To get more badges in Girl Guides.
- Stop talking in class.
- To be able to play the "SpongeBob" theme on the piano.
- To stay fit.
- To have a good summer.
- To have a fun birthday party.
- Keep my closet clean.
- Keep my desk clean.
- Get more I Did It Awards.
- Run for thirty minutes without stopping.
- Have a great last month of the school year.

To increase successful goal completion, students needed to visualize their goal. They needed to see themselves completing the goal and receiving its benefits.

The more powerful the visualizing, the more likely a successful goal.[36][37][38] After one month, I reviewed the goals individually with students. After the review, I gave them another sheet for the next month's goal.[39]

Each of us has twenty-four hours a day, or 1,440 minutes, or 86,400 seconds every day to use. How we use them determines our success.

NEXT STEPS:

1. Make copies of the Goal Setting handout for your class in the *How to Succeed as an Elementary Teacher Workbook* (found here: http://thebusyeducator.com/succeednow).

2. Develop a lesson plan to introduce the Goal Setting handout.

3. Collect and read the student goals.

4. Post the student goals on the bulletin board.

5. Interview students once a month after their goal sheet is handed back.

How To Achieve Excellence

*"You cannot help someone get up a hill
without getting closer to the top yourself."*

General H. Norman Schwarzkopf

To achieve excellence, students need to know what it is. When new students enter my room, they see above the front board my "I Did It Awards" posted from the year before. These awards are printed in color on stock paper.

A reproducible copy of the I Did It Award can be found in the
How to Succeed as an Elementary Teacher Workbook
(found here:http://thebusyeducator.com/succeednow).

I explain to my new students that one of my goals is to have every student in the class earn an I Did It Award. When a student achieves excellence, they receive this award. Earning it can be for many accomplishments: perfect tests, perfect attendance, dramatic improvement in behavior and attitude, being the most improved student of the month, exceptional improvement in a school subject, first student in a physical education class to run twenty minutes without stopping, most improved in reading and writing, etc.

The appeal of the award is that it is special. It is not given out for something that anyone can do. For example, students will often ask if they will receive an I Did It Award for passing a particularly easy review test. I tell them, "No. It's not challenging enough for the award."

So the award is very appealing and motivating, particularly to my high-achieving students. In feedback I receive from my high-achieving students, they rate this award as a top motivator in my class. They rate it highly because it is a special award that not everyone can get every time. I also make the award special by having a mini-award ceremony. I call up each student, shake their hand, and congratulate them on earning the I Did It Award. I then get the entire class to acknowledge the achievement by a round of applause.

The award is also very appealing to my special-needs students and students with low self-confidence and self-esteem. By having the previous year's awards posted above the front board, students can see who earned it the year before.[40] They see students they know who aren't strong academically, but have achieved success. The award is set up to give all students a place, all students hope and encouragement, all students a chance to achieve excellence. I believe every student comes to class with at least one strength. It may not be self-evident, but the strength is there. It's my job to find, note it and strengthen it, and celebrate it. The I Did It Award does that!

Building Good Public Relations—One Kitchen at a Time

The very first time that a student gets a perfect mark for a unit math test, I print out two I Did It Awards. One of the awards is posted above the front board for everyone to see.

The other award is a keeper award. I tell the student to put it on their refrigerator. By having the award on the refrigerator, the student sees a solid reminder of excellence and success every day. Imagine having ten to fifteen students getting an I Did It Award. The award builds up a sense of accomplishment, class morale, and self-esteem. It builds your own sense of accomplishment.

Nothing succeeds like success. Success breeds success. Parents too are proud to see the award and they encourage their children to keep up their excellent work. Family members, family friends, and visitors who come into the kitchen also see the award. Often they make a comment to the child about his or her achievement. Students also go away with a solid example of how to achieve excellence and success. They also see the rewards that come with them. The other tangible benefits are the positives that reflect on you as a teacher and on the school itself. Our teaching and educational system can only get better whenever we can bring the positives to the homes of our students and their families.

How many awards can a student earn? The more the better. Some of my high-achieving students have earned over twenty. Some of my below-average students have earned only one. However, only their first award is posted. All students are equal above that front board. Later awards are their keepers for home. Once their refrigerator at home gets overcrowded with awards, some of my students put them into their albums and scrapbooks.

Another way to show students success is to allow them to know more about you. A number of teachers have a bulletin board or corner of the classroom showing their personal side. This may consist of a class photos of kindergarten, high school, university graduation photos, sports teams, and wedding and family pictures.

On my bulletin board, I post the awards that took me years to achieve. They are my university degrees. Students need a visual reminder that their teacher has achieved success and excellence too!

And, perhaps that they have overcome some failure as well. For example, I tell them of how I failed at French, but after high school, I went on to live with a French-speaking family for three summers and I started to really enjoy the language and culture. This kind of sharing is an encouragement to students and can give them hope.

NEXT STEPS:

1. Decide on whether you want to implement an awards system for your class.

2. Brainstorm a list of accomplishments you want to award.

3. Use the I Did It Award template in the *How to Succeed as an Elementary Teacher Workbook* (found here: http://thebusyeducator.com/succeednow) or design your own.

Chapter 2:
Reinforcing the Foundation

Planning to Plan

"Success consists of moving from failure to failure without losing heart."

Winston Churchill

With your foundation set, now you can build upon and reinforce it with a student planner.

A student planner can teach and strengthen:

- Time management.
- Study skills.
- Organizational skills.
- Problem solving.
- Tracking reading.
- Building friendships.
- Reinforcing neat writing.
- Learning responsibility.
- Home-school communication (between home room teacher and rotary teachers).
- Parental support.

All these skills aren't going to be taught all at once, of course. As your students learn to use their planners, you will be introducing these skills one at a time. However, you will reinforce them all year long.

Over the years, I have either made my own or purchased commercial planners. I prefer the commercial planners. They save time and are expertly done. There are many companies in the planner business. There are also electronic planners.[41] [42] I preferred to use paper.

Costs vary depending on the number of planners bought. The schools where I have taught usually ask parents to contribute part of the fee. They also ask the Home and School or Parent Teacher Association to contribute part of the fee as well. It's a crucial investment for parents and students, and for you, the teacher.

Planner Secrets

The key to using a planner is consistency. Use it daily for it to be effective. Since parents and the PTA have contributed their hard-earned money to buy the planners, they want to know that students are using it.

You can plant the seeds of parental and community support by using it. This will go a long way in building a supportive and positive relationship with parents when they see their children using the planners.

If it's not being used consistently, parents may become resentful. They may think twice about giving you or the school financial support. It's the little things that count next time you ask them!

Its use by students must be reinforced as well. If not, they won't take it seriously. And if students don't take it seriously, you will be trying to cope with lost or forgotten planners all year long.

Over the years, I've found that every student will still have their planners if I do the following: consistently check their planners; reward students for bringing them in; and reward them for having their homework assignments written down, completed, and then signed by their parents.

We also do a scavenger type of activity to teach all the major sections of the planner. This will depend on the planner you use. For example, I hand out a sheet that asks students to answer questions from the major sections of the planner. In this way they get familiar with their planner in a fun way.

In my early years, I never would have thought it possible to have students hold onto something like a planner all year long. If you take the time and effort to make using the planner important, your students will make it important as well.

Using a Planner Successfully

There are many ways to use the planner. I introduce its use as soon as I receive them. I begin by making sure students neatly print or write their name, address, and homeroom teacher in their planners.

I also make sure students have written down the names, phone numbers, and e-mail addresses of at least two students in the class as their "study buddies". I tell them they can use their "study buddies" not just for homework, but also information about activities in and out of school. There will be a number of special activities such as parties, Tie Day, Hat Day, and Beach Day. If they have been absent from school, they will miss out on them when they come back unless they keep in touch with their study buddies.

I also stress that it's their responsibility to contact their study buddies for missed homework, assignments, and news. It is not their study buddies' responsibility to contact them. I also tell them they can keep in touch in person, by phone, by e-mail, and by text.

Using a Planner to Build Class Community

Having students write down the names of at least two study buddies is the start of networking and of relationship building. It is also one way of observing the class dynamics. You can quickly discover the popular students and their group of friends. Also, you can find out quickly the students who may need some help in finding and forming friendships. It's also something to draw to the attention of parents during interviews and to note when forming classes for next year. I tried to make sure every student has at least one friend in their class for next year.

Planner Routines

There are many ways to reinforce the use of the planner. Depending on my class schedule, I would use five to ten minutes at the end of the day as planner time. On the front board I wrote down the homework assignments for the day. I included a minimum of twenty minutes of reading out loud or quiet reading at home. I made sure to ask students if they had any homework assignments, tests, or projects from classes that I didn't teach: music, science and technology, etc.

I asked students to tell me one thing they learned in class that day. I liked to do this before lunch and before the end-of-the-day dismissal. Doing so gave students something to tell their parents when they are asked, "What did you do in school today?" I had students write this down in their planners.

I wrote down on chart paper any new words or concepts they discovered. This is to review and reinforce what they learned that day. This is also a great way to show parents that their child is actually learning and remembering what was taught in school. Before students head out for home, I also stapled into their planners important handouts that their parents needed to read and sign.

I also used the planner as a communication tool with parents. I did this by writing a note to parents and/or stapling personal letters or the class newsletter into the planner for parents to read. I also encouraged parents to write me notes if there was something I needed to know about their child. This could be anything from difficulty with a homework assignment, an upcoming absence, or times and dates for a meeting with them. I found when things are written down, there was less chance for miscommunication between home and school.

Getting the Planner from School to Home and Back

Here's a great way to encourage a student to take home a planner every night: write something positive about the student in the planner for the parent to see. By that point, I'd usually identified two or three students who had a troubled past. As soon as they did something positive, I made sure to note it in the planner.

Some teachers prefer to check each planner before students leave for the day. Others do it in the morning. I checked the planners before students left and I checked them before they entered class or first thing in the morning. I checked to see that the homework assignment on the board was written down. I checked that there was a parent signature or initial indicating to me that the parent had seen the assignment and planner. I also checked to see if the number of reading minutes had been recorded and if they had written down at least one new thing they learned in class that day. Again, depending on your planner, you may only have room for the homework assignment and reading minutes. Planners are constantly changing and some years they have more, sometimes less room for personal notes.

To confirm clarity, I used the "alien test". Could an "alien" or stranger read what is written down? Or, if three of your classmates can't read what you wrote, you're not communicating well. Sometimes I would go into another class, or asked a student passing by in the hallway to read what the student had written. If this student couldn't read what was written down in the planner, the planner fails the "alien test". This strategy is one way of reinforcing neatness and clear communication. Parents, too, may comment in the planner if their child's writing is sloppy or neat!

What? No Planner!

What if the student doesn't have his or her planner? Accept no excuses. There are students who have learned over the years to have a good excuse ready. They will talk your ear off with it. I simply and calmly asked them, "How do you plan to make sure it's here tomorrow?" This question catches students off guard. They've been working on using their excuse with you because they think they're going to get into trouble with you (this is an opportunity to teach and develop problem solving with the students. If I see a pattern in the number of students not having their planners complete, we discuss as a class some solutions to the problem. Doing so may simply be a matter of putting the planner on the kitchen table every night before going to bed, or asking a parent to sign it first thing in the morning. Your class will come up with many other innovative solutions.).

As I checked the planners, I would put a mark beside their name on my clipboard list if they don't have it signed. There would be consequences if students didn't have their planner or if their planner was incomplete three times in a week. I enrolled them in "The Club". This is one club I told students they do not want to join! I would put their names in my notepad and I kept them after school. I would check not only their planner, but also all their work in all their notebooks. This included subjects I didn't teach that day. If anything is not done, they needed to work on it before going home. Membership in The Club rarely lasted more than a week.

A roll of "gotcha's" from Staples.

If a student had a complete planner, I gave them two "gotchas" ("gotchas" are admit-one tickets or coupons that I bought from a stationary or office supply store such as Staples. They come in single rolls of five hundred tickets, or a double roll of one thousand tickets. I've used my own in the past, but the commercial ones save a lot of time and energy. This is one of my incentive programs. I'll describe other incentive programs in the next chapter.).

When I gave a "gotcha" to students, they immediately printed their names on the ticket. They kept them in their desks until I collected all the tickets.

I gave one for their parent's signature and one for having taken down the assignment. I found that every student should be able to take down the assignment at the end of the day.

Getting a parent's signature can be a bit more difficult, especially if the parent works nights and doesn't get to see the student after school. That's the point where the class brainstorms ways of getting that signature. Sometimes the answer is a matter of training the parent!

NEXT STEPS:

1. Find out if your school has a planner system in place.

2. Decide on a paper planner, electronic planner, or combination of both.

3. Print out the Planner Checklist found in the *How to Succeed as an Elementary Teacher Workbook* (found here: http://thebusyeducator.com/succeednow).

4. Decide whether you will be rewarding students for completing their planners.

Motivating Your Class

"A word of encouragement during a failure
is worth more than an hour of praise after success."

Anonymous

Nothing ever goes smoothly all the time. Every foundation starts to have some cracks. There are many ways to avoid these cracks in your classes' learning journey. Certainly, you need to be flexible and "go with the flow" in the class. Use variety to spice up your teaching and make the day go quicker. "All work and no play makes Jack a dull boy", after all.

One of the best ways to avoid the cracks in your journey of daily teaching is through an incentive system or reward program. I have already discussed one such program in the previous chapter.[43] [44]

A number of factors determine the success of an effective incentive program:

- Have a valid purpose for it.
- Target only the behaviors you want to reinforce.
- Do not reinforce behaviors you don't want.
- Students need to know how it works.
- Keep it simple.
- Make managing it simple, too.
- Make sure you and your students are comfortable with it.
- Have more than one incentive program throughout the year or at one time.

Every year has its unique challenges. Every class is different. What works one year may not work the next year and vice versa. Decide on a system for the entire class and a system for individual students.

My I Did It Award is an incentive designed to target excellence and doing one's best. Although it is an individual award, it's set up so that every student in the class is able to earn an award by year's end.[45]

Incentive Systems[46]

When I began teaching students in both regular and special education classes, I used a chart and star system. I used it to track certain behaviors which I knew every student could achieve. I focused on behaviors such as bringing in forms and tests that needed to be signed by parents, completing homework assignments, quietly working on tasks at a class center, and on class/individual projects.

Each time a student completed a certain activity, I handed out a gold star and had the students put them beside their names on the chart. Students competed to see who would be first to get to the end of the chart. When the "winning" student got to the end of the chart, I rewarded him or her with a small prize. I then waited until all the others caught up. Once everyone in the class got to the end, I would take the chart and hang it up on the wall. It was an impressive sight, having a Bristol board chart filled with hundreds of gold stars. By the end of the year, these charts filled with gold stars surrounded the class.

This was a very successful tracking and incentive system. What I found very interesting was that students knew who would be the first to complete the chart and "win". Students who knew they couldn't "win" and compete with the best student in the class would compete against a friend or someone that was on the same level as themselves. This proved to be a "win-win" system, since I didn't finish the chart until every student made it to the end and the whole class was rewarded.

Although this system did what it was designed to do for the type of classes I was teaching at the time, over the years I learned to try other systems as well. Using variety not only keeps students interested, but it also keeps you motivated too!

Using "Gotchas"

I had many incentive programs in my classes. I used "gotchas" to track completion of planners. All the skills I was trying to teach through the use of the planner were (and are!) very important. Completing their planners and managing their planners is the only way students can earn "gotchas".

Of course, you can use "gotchas" to target other class and individual behaviors. In my case, every two weeks we collected the "gotchas" and put them into a box. I used a clipboard with a class list while I called out the names of each student, so that I could record their number of "gotchas". I used this number for our school color house incentive system. I awarded points to each student, as well for their color house. By tracking the points, I learned the number of times students completed their planners for the month. I also learn how responsible students had been in keeping their "gotchas".

Every two weeks in the last month of school, for the last ten minutes on a Friday afternoon, I drew names from the box. Over the years, I have used all kinds of prizes as incentives, from books, stationery and trading cards, candy, chocolate bars, and potato chips! Throughout my teaching, I've noticed that it isn't the prize that motivates students; rather, *winning* the prize is the motivator. I have made the same observation with teachers, whether awarded door prizes or other draws at staff functions. People don't care as much about what they win, as long as they win something! My teenage daughter has confirmed this too. She told me that "it doesn't matter what I win, as long as I win something!"

With that in mind, I now give out a sucker or a lollipop. I tell students that the only prize I give out is a lollipop or sucker. It doesn't matter. Students are thrilled to win something.

Once I draw students' names, they pick a prize, but they need to say "Thank you" before I give it to them. It's an opportunity to reinforce good manners, which I find are sometimes lacking among some students. As soon as the time is up (or as soon as the bell rings) the draw is over, providing me an opportunity to reinforce the importance of time. Everything has to come to an end.

The Points Incentive System

Another incentive system I used involved points. Points are easy to manage and easy for students to understand. I explained to them how I get points by using my credit card for paying my bills and for buying groceries. They too can earn points. You can decide what behaviors to target and the number of points to award. There are no limits to the type or variety of rewards you can give. They may be a short field trip, a movie, an end-of-the-term party, free time, no homework, extra recess, extra physical education class, or the like.

Some teachers aim for 100% compliance of all students before awarding points. Others choose a lesser percentage. If there are one or two students who try to sabotage the group efforts of the class, they can be counseled privately or excluded from taking part in the reward activity.

I usually used a small area on my back blackboard to keep a running total of the class points. In addition to having a running total of points, I liked to link the points to a sentence such as "Let's Go Celebrate Now!" that the class needed to complete to get the reward. Then I could teach some math by asking students how much is each letter worth (five points) and how many points they needed to complete the sentence (one hundred points). I could also add in my English lesson and tell them that the apostrophe (') and exclamation mark (!) are important and count for points as well!

Still another incentive system used by teachers is the granting of personal time or personal activity time. This is a period of time, usually a half hour, that students can use for personal activities (reading their favorite book or magazine, drawing, working on the computer, going to the library, playing a board game with a friend, or going to another class as a peer tutor or buddy). Students can also catch up on any work they missed during the week. I liked to use part of the time to have students clean and organize their desks. If they take the time to clean and organize their desks beforehand, then they can have the whole period for their own personal use.

Once the personal activity time is over, students put away the games, books, and magazines. They shut down the computers. I would stand at the door, wish each and every student a good weekend, and give them a "high five". It's a fantastic way to end the week and to begin the weekend on a positive note.

Bonus Bucks Auction Incentive System

After a long cold winter and a rainy spring, the last month of school finds my students very restless. They are excited to be outside again playing in the warm sunshine. It's a challenging time to motivate them to do work.

A fellow staff member told me about the bonus bucks auction. It is a special auction that can take place at any time. Usually it is left for the last month of school.

The bonus bucks look like Monopoly money. Some teachers buy these bucks at a games store. Others make their own. They hand out these bucks similar to the way I hand out my "gotchas". I replaced the bonus bucks with my "gotchas". Each "gotcha" is worth $10.

Auction Procedures:

1. Secretary (and helper) count out "gotchas" received by each student.
2. Secretary records number of "gotchas" on class list and multiplies totals by ten.
3. Bidding in increments of $10.
4. No sharing or splitting of bids.
5. Secretary records winning bid amounts on class list.
6. Some prizes are subject to a reserve bid.
7. Students to check in and pay secretary BEFORE claiming prize.
8. Auction can end at ANY time!

Items to be Auctioned:

1. Permission to chew gum for entire day.
2. Use of Mr. Glavac's wheelie chair (three available for auction).
3. Pick your own seat for the day.
4. Pencils.
5. Pencil sharpeners.
6. Free time in computer lab for entire class (Reserve bid $1000).
7. Movie for class (Reserve bid $500).
8. Extended recess (Reserve bid $500).
9. Free choice for gym period.
10. No homework pass.
11. Permission to wear your hat in class for the day.
12. Hat day for the class (Reserve bid $1000).
13. Sit anywhere for one week.
14. Candy/chips/donuts.
15. Teacher for one period.
16. Priority pass for dismissal at the end of the day.

17. Choice of classroom jobs.

18. Pick order of subjects taught for the day.

19. Popcorn for class.

20. Mystery package.

Have fun!

NEXT STEPS:

1. Decide on whether you want to implement an incentive system.

2. List the behaviors you want to target.

3. Introduce and teach the procedures.

4. Give the bonus bucks auction system a try. It's a lot of fun!

5. See the *How to Succeed as an Elementary Teacher Workbook* (found here: http://thebusyeducator.com/succeednow) for certificate template to print out.

Winning Strategies

"Nothing great was ever achieved without enthusiasm."

Ralph Waldo Emerson

The first major assignment I have students do during the first week of school is the "Time Capsule". I would hand this assignment out on the first day of school. Giving this assignment so early immediately reinforces that we will be doing work in class and that the emphasis is on learning. You can easily modify this assignment so that all students are able to do it.

And if, as some have said, that students only remember their first and last days of school, then let's give them something to remember.

The Time Capsule gives students a sense of achievement and success at the outset of that first week. The subjects are personal and relevant to every student. There are no wrong answers. And, since we will have been working on all the topics during the first day, it's a guarantee of success!

It's also an assignment that shows students a sense of time, change, and history, since they will open these time capsules on the very last day of school.

Procedure

I asked students to bring in a number of items in a "time capsule" container (shoe box, plastic container, manila envelope, etc.). These will hold items such as a list of students' favorite things: TV shows, movies, recording artists, songs, books, subjects, colors, friends, foods, hobbies, etc. I then asked for a piece of string measuring their height, a copy of their handprint and footprint on a piece of paper, a flower or leaf wrapped in plastic wrap, and a list of three goals that they want to accomplish by the end of the school year.

On the Friday or the following Monday, I had students present their time capsules to the class. I photographed each student with a digital camera and then videotaped the presentation. Since the photographs were digital, I saved them to the computer hard drive. I then used this photograph for their I Did It Awards and for their birthday cards. I also printed out all the students' photos with their names underneath for substitute teachers. You can also use a class seating plan with the children's photos above their names (a great help to supply teachers).

Time Capsule

Purpose: A lot of changes will occur between your first day of school in September (August) and your last day of school in June. To see some of those changes, we will be making individualized 'time capsules."

Please supply **a** "time capsule" container (shoe box, plastic container, manila envelope etc.) to hold the following items:

- A headline from this week's newspaper, radio, TV, Internet news.
- An article from the newspaper or from your favorite magazine or from the Internet,
- A list of your favorite things such as: TV shows, movies, recording artists, songs, books, subjects, colors, friends, foods, hobbies, etc.
- A flower or leaf wrapped in plastic wrap.
- An example of your handwriting.
- Your handprint on a piece of paper.
- Your footprint on a piece of paper.
- Your weight.
- A piece of string measuring your height.
- A paragraph {100-150) words describing your class and your teacher.
- A recent photograph.
- A list of 3 goals you want to accomplish by the end of the school year.

Due Date _____

**Be prepared to preseut your "time capsule" iu frout of the class
for a videotaped presentation**

The Time Capsule handout is available from the
How to Succeed as an Elementary Teacher Workbook
(found here: http://thebusyeducator.com/succeednow).

For their videotaped presentation, I had them introduce themselves. They then picked three things from their time capsule to present. I collected the time capsules and told the students that the capsules will be "buried". I would usually put them in the basement, crawl space, or closet, and they wouldn't see them until the last day of school.

Time Capsule Extensions

- Divide students into groups of four.
- Have students practice presenting their time capsules to each other.
- In their Learning Logs, have students write one thing they learned about their group members.
- Have students list ten objects in the classroom that are shorter than the string used to measure their height in their Learning Logs.
- Have students list ten objects in the classroom that are taller than the string used to measure their height in their Learning Logs.
- Have students guess how much taller they will be at the end of the school year and write this prediction in their Learning Logs.
- Have students go into the hallway and put the strings in order from longest to shortest.
- Find a person who is closest to their height and write their name in their Learning Logs.

From this assignment, you can quickly get a handle on how responsible each student is (if they can't hand this assignment in, they're going to have a tough time handing in other assignments!). There are no wrong answers here. With this assignment, they show how creative they are, their work habits, and their presentation skills. The Time Capsule assignment also gives you marks and comments for their report cards. This assignment generates marks and comments for oral presentation skills, reading, and writing (see the Time Capsule Rubric in the *How to Succeed as an Elementary Teacher Workbook (found here:* http://thebusyeducator.com/succeednow).

Before I "buried" the time capsules, I would include a letter in the future to the student. This is an example of what students will read on the last day of school:

> Dear Billy,
>
> Thank you for your Time Capsule. I enjoyed reading it.
>
> Today is October 18. When you read these words, it will be the last day of school in June.
>
> I hope you had a great year in Grade 6. I always enjoy listening to your answers because they are "right on" and "out of the box".

All the best for next year.

Have a safe and wonderful summer,

M. Glavac

It's a good idea to check the time capsules before putting them away. I looked for anything that might spoil such as fruit, vegetables, cookies, cake, etc. It's amazing what some students will wrap up in plastic wrap!

Be sure to exclude these at the outset.

At the end of their video presentation, I had every student fill out a "Fan Mail" (they handed these in to me. I made sure to read them over to make sure there is nothing inappropriate written on them.). I then gave them to the student presenter.

Imagine what it's like for a student to receive positive comments from all their fellow students; and all from their first presentation in your class! Imagine if it's a student with poor self-esteem. This is a simple but powerful strategy. You will be building up rapport and positive connections among your students. You will also be showing students how to show their appreciation and respect for something that is done for them.

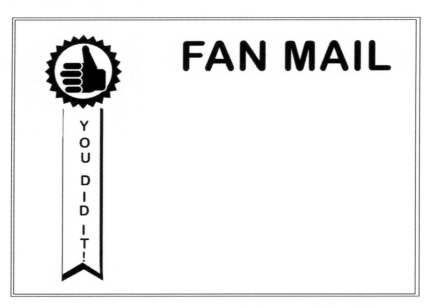

The "Fan Mail" certificate template is available in the
How to Succeed as an Elementary Teacher Workbook
(found here: http://thebusyeducator.com/succeednow).

Other activities for students to find out more about themselves and each other are autobiographies, silhouettes[47], life maps[48] [49], timelines, "A Day in My Life", etc.

Post the students' work so that the projects surround your class in time for Meet the Teacher Night.

NEXT STEPS:

1. Print out the Time Capsule handout from the *How to Succeed as an Elementary Teacher Workbook* (found here: http://thebusyeducator.com/succeednow).

2. Have some extra shoeboxes or manila envelopes on hand for students who don't have a time capsule container.

3. Print out enough "Fan Mail" certificates from the *How to Succeed as an Elementary Teacher Workbook* for students in your class.

4. Print out the Time Capsule Presentation Rubric handout from the *How to Succeed as an Elementary Teacher Workbook* if students are being marked on their presentation.

5. Bring camera and video camera to film student presentations.

6. Print out the Time Capsule Extension: The Metric Me handout from the *How to Succeed as an Elementary Teacher Workbook*.

7. Before "burying" the time capsules, check them for anything that may spoil such as fruit, vegetables, cookies, cake, etc.

Connecting Students With Others: Expanding a Student's Circle of Influence

*"We might cease thinking of school as a place, and learn to believe that it is basically relationships between children and adults, and between children and other children.
The four walls and the principal's office would cease to loom so hugely as the essential ingredients."*

George Dennision

Painlessly Picking Groups

Once students had a good grasp of who they were, I started connecting and showing them how to network with each other. Do this on the very first day by using the scavenger hunt. It is also done by putting students into groups.

I used groups for every subject. Most groups are temporary; some are permanent. For the making of temporary groups, I used a plastic container with pupil names from a class list. I randomly picked the names for partners and for groups. I also used this method to pick who goes first in a game or a presentation. This way, I avoided all kinds of arguments. Random selection also ties in very well if you're doing a lesson on probability. For example, I'd ask the class, "There are thirty names in the container. I pull ten names but I haven't pulled yours yet. What is the probability that yours will be next?"

Students sometimes dread being in a group with specific students. I avoided a lot of drama by telling them how long the group will be together. It may be for only ten or twenty minutes. I told them, "You're not marrying the person, just working together to solve a problem, like in the real world." I also told them that there are times that I have been in a group with a person I didn't get along. Usually I found out something interesting about that person that I didn't know.

Here is a good way of building group harmony among students with weak social skills: the interview question. As an icebreaker and to build up rapport, I had students introduce themselves to someone they didn't know in the group. Then I had them all ask each other a question before they worked on an assignment. It can be something like, "What is one thing you will be doing on the weekend?"[50] or "What is your favorite book, song, movie, T.V. show?"

As they were working on the assignment, I went around and talked to group members. I asked, "What is one thing you found out about the other people in your group?" I also used this approach when I assigned a new class seating plan. After a seating change, I had students interview their classmates who are seated around them. In this way, students in the class will get to know other students in the class whom they may yet know. I wanted students to know the names of all their classmates. I also wanted them to know at least one, two, or three things about them before the end of the year.

Group Success Strategies

Another key to group success is making the groups last for a short time. Ten to twenty minutes is a good period of time for students to get to know each other. This lessens the opportunity to get into too many arguments!

Sending groups to different areas of the class or school can make a big difference in how groups operate. It can also make a difference on the quality and quantity of material that comes back. First, make sure you know which students can be responsible outside the classroom. Some of my students would lose this privilege for inappropriate actions. The next time we did groups, they needed more direct supervision.

Another factor to keep in mind for group success is to have clear and easily achievable goals. This is especially important at the beginning of the year. Outline the goals for all students before they're put into groups.

Predicting Group Dynamics

For groups that need to be yearlong, such as in reading and phys. ed., or for seating groups of three to four weeks, I would sometimes do a sociogram exercise.

This sociogram can be as simple or as detailed as you like. I liked to ask the following questions to get a good idea about who my students were. On a piece of paper, I asked students to answer these three statements:

1. I would like to sit with this person:

   First Choice _____

   Second Choice _____

   Third Choice _____

2. If I needed help for a class assignment, I would ask:

   First Choice _____

   Second Choice _____

   Third Choice _____

3. I would play on a sports team with this student:

   First Choice _____

   Second Choice _____

   Third Choice _____

Record the data on a class list or on a spreadsheet. With this information, you can use a software application to simplify the diagraming. From these three questions, I got a good idea about the social, intellectual, and physical abilities of students. It's a great exercise to see who the leaders are in social, academic, and athletic areas in the class. It also pinpoints which students may need support in those areas.

Connecting Students One-on-One

Another way I started connecting and showing students how to network with each other is through in-depth interviews.

Students chose a partner to interview (sometimes I would pull names randomly to decide on partners). I handed out the "Interview Form" (see the *How to Succeed as an Elementary Teacher Workbook*

(found here: http://thebusyeducator.com/succeednow)

and allowed time in class for students to interview each other.

Extensions

You can choose to have students work on their presentation skills by having them present their interview partners to the class. Limit the presentation to five to seven questions.

Another activity you may want to try is a "Who Am I?" guessing game. This is a mystery-type game where I picked five questions about a mystery student. The students tried to guess who the mystery student was. Once I revealed the mystery student, I had the student's photograph and their interview form posted on our bulletin board.

After students learned how to interview each other, I had them interview teachers, administration, support staff, and parent volunteers. This is a great way to connect them to people they see every day.

Another extension of this activity is one I used in social studies/civics classes. I researched the names and phone numbers of each of the trustee members of our district board of education. The class brainstormed on the questions we wanted to ask of each of the trustees. Students were then paired with a trustee member for a phone interview. Before the phone interview, we did mock interviews in class to practice.

I also extended an invitation to the trustees to come into our class and do a presentation on what they do. This offered students more opportunity to practice their interviewing skills. They also learned to thank and acknowledge the trustee for taking the time to come to our class.

Buddy Program

By far the most important activity I did to connect with others is the Buddy Program. Early in the year I asked teachers if I could match up or buddy up my class with their class. Sometimes they approached and ask me. It's a great way for students to act as mentors for students in lower grades. It builds self-esteem and confidence in students. I usually had my class become buddies with another class for a thirty-minute period once a week. During this time, we shared many activities: reading, writing, artwork, science projects, and/or sports activities.

There are a number of benefits for teachers. For myself, I got to know students in kindergarten five years before I got to teach them in fifth grade. They also got to know me. I have used eighth grade students to help log the kindergarten students into their computers. I have also used fifth grade students to teach primary students how to skate by pushing them in chairs around an ice rink.

In one of my schools, we had a class for developmentally disabled students. This class had a number of students in wheelchairs. I would often have four to six students go to the class to help the teacher once a week for thirty minutes. This activity is a great opportunity for my students to socialize with other students who are different from themselves. They also learned how to assist them. I also had students volunteer for their former teachers. They did this during their personal activity time on Friday afternoons.

This is a great opportunity for students who may have behavioral difficulties. One year, I had two students who had a long history of fighting, aggression, and anger control issues. To help them learn to control this behavior, I had them go to the kindergarten room every afternoon, an hour before dismissal. Once there, they would do activities with the kindergarten children and assist the teacher with dismissal. Their help was much appreciated by the teacher. It was especially appreciated on cold winter days when the children needed to put on their heavy coats, boots, mittens, and hats. They also helped to pack up their knapsacks and put in them any handouts and projects going home! The responsibility of helping others had an amazing effect on the two students. They calmed down before their own dismissal from my class.

Students also worked in pairs or groups outside the classroom to plant trees, tend the school gardens, and clean up the schoolyard. Other projects involved visits to senior citizens' homes, hosting senior's visits to the school, and writing family and community biographies. You will have other excellent ideas for such relationship and building with your class.

Every activity outside the classroom is ideal to photograph and videotape. You can submit stories for newsletters, memory books, or class writing assignments. These activities contribute to your class climate, culture, team building, and a sense of belonging.

The Kindergarten Buddy Program

For a number of years, my class was buddied with a kindergarten class.

My students interviewed their class buddies for a superhero story, starring their buddies as the superhero. They created a storyboard and summary of the story, and typed up the story and presented it to their buddies just before the holiday break (see the *How to Succeed as an Elementary Teacher Workbook*

(found here: http://thebusyeducator.com/succeednow).

for the Kindergarten superhero story buddy project checklist and storyboard).

The most professionally fulfilling project we did one year with our kindergarten buddies was around phonological awareness[51].

The kindergarten teacher had developed many phonological awareness activities, and she taught my students how to teach them to their buddies. Once a week throughout the school year, my students worked with their buddies teaching phonological awareness.

The results were astounding:

Phonological Awareness Screening 2009–2010

Thames Valley District School Board

Average score out of 66: **Fall = 33.0**
Spring = 49.9
Change = 16.9

Percentage of Students Designated as "Have Skill": **Fall = 50%**
Spring = 76%
Change = 26%

Buddy Class

Average score out of 66: **Fall = 30.0**
Spring = 57.5
Change = 27.5

Percentage of Students Designated as "Have Skill": **Fall = 12.5%**
Spring = 87%
Change = 74.5%

This shows that students helping students can make a big difference.

NEXT STEPS:

1. Use a plastic container with pupil names from a class list or a computer random generator program to select groups.

2. If using the sociogram for selecting groups, review procedure and recommended software applications.

3. To connect students one-on-one through interviews, print and hand out the interview form from the *How to Succeed as an Elementary Teacher Workbook* (found here: http://thebusyeducator.com/succeednow).

4. Consider doing a buddy program with another teacher colleague.

5. See the on-one through interviews, print and hand out the interview form from the *How to Succeed as an Elementary Teacher Workbook* for the kindergarten superhero story buddy project checklist and storyboard.

Getting Outside Help to Connect Students to Others

"Many hands lighten the load"

Chinese Proverb

One thing you will learn quickly as a teacher is that you can't do everything. You don't have the time, resources, or skills to be perfect. You can only do the best you can. A popular saying goes, "Perfection is the enemy of excellence". One advantage of knowing who you are is the ability to complement your weaknesses and use your strengths. You might also want to connect students with other people outside your class who have the strengths that you lack.

I have little to no art ability. Fortunately, when I was teaching there were a number of staff members who loved art and enjoyed teaching it. One way to bring in another staff member to teach your class is to combine classes. You become the helper and the other staff member is the expert; in this case, the art expert.

Another way is to trade classes. I've gone into primary classes to teach about bees (I used to be a part-time beekeeper), and at the same time the kindergarten teacher has gone into my class to teach art lessons.

Exchanges are win-win opportunities for teachers and students. Students win by connecting with other staff members. They discover and enjoy the benefits of that teacher's strengths and interests. The expert staff member wins by having you teach their class a subject in which you have a strength, or have a great desire to teach. They also win when they reconnect with students they may have taught years ago, or when they want to try out a different teaching assignment with a different age range of students. You win because you also connect with another class, and with students that you may be teaching a year or so down the road. Of course, you get to teach a subject that you're an expert in and enjoy doing, too.

Connecting Students and Community

I've also used this strategy to connect students with their community. In the early days of computers and the Internet, I wanted to integrate these new technologies into my class. I wanted to show students how to create webpages. Unfortunately, I knew very little about creating webpages and I didn't have the time to learn how to create them.

I contacted the local university by sending my request in an e-mail to a student list. Within days, I received dozens of replies. I found two excellent students. They came into my class and volunteered hundreds of hours of their time to work with my students to produce webpages from their work. I gave the volunteers excellent references to future employers. My students received expert instruction on new computer technology.

My former school takes this idea to a higher level. In the beginning of the school year, the resource team goes to the local university to recruit student volunteers. There are so many volunteers that the administration rents a school bus to bring them into the school. A "volunteer fair" is set up in the gym to pair volunteer with teachers. This is done after school where teachers set up a desk advertising their requirements. These university volunteers staff our entire after-school homework program. It's a win-win situation for everyone: older students fulfill volunteer requirements for their program, and the school gets extra help for students.

Another great resource are high school students. They could be your former students. So, too, are parents[52]. Some schools have a database of parents and their skills, which teachers may access. There is also a Speakers Bureau for other professionals such as doctors, lawyers, engineers, and dentists. During a mystery unit, I invited my dentist to talk about forensics and how dentists identify criminals through their dental work.

Before you use any volunteers, however, make sure you are clear on your school and district's volunteer policies. Some districts require a police check, the completion of special forms, and the briefing of volunteers on procedures of confidentiality.

NEXT STEPS:

1. Find a staff member that you can work with.

2. Decide on exchanging or combining classes to teach a lesson.

3. Contact your local university, college, and/or high school for classroom volunteers.

4. Check with your administration for guidelines, i.e. police background checks, for volunteers and confidentiality procedures.

Building Trust and Respect through Responsibility

"Earn trust, earn trust, earn trust. Then you can worry about the rest."

Seth Godin

"You have to create a culture where everybody has an opportunity to be recognized."

John Mackey

To have trusting, respectful, and responsible students, they need to be trusted with responsibility. One of the best ways to do this is to give students a meaningful job to do in the class. In the past, I would often assign jobs to students, but they wouldn't do them.

This frustrated me. I often resented the lack of respect and responsibility shown. This led in turn to me not trusting students to carry out their responsibilities. Over the years, I've found many keys to make the assigning of jobs work well:

- Let students choose their jobs. Students who are motivated to take on responsibilities will more than likely do a better job than those who aren't.
- Use a fair and equitable way to hand out the jobs.
- Make sure there is a variety of jobs available.
- Make the jobs important.
- Train students how to do the job properly.[53]
- Have students who have done a job train their replacements.

Ensuring a Successful Job System

Once my students started to get settled into the classroom routines and procedures, I would take out my list of jobs. They ranged from handling the attendance folder and audio-visual equipment to recording points and being the class secretary. I posted the jobs with names of students beside each job. The key to success is to have a system for changing jobs. This ensures every student has an equal and fair chance to get the job they want.

Once a month, I devoted a period of class time for the assigning of jobs. The very first time I did this, I would number and put every job on my list on the board. Beside the list, I would put the number of people needed to do the job. I used my container of names to randomly pick students. As I pulled each name, I asked that student which job they wanted to do and I recorded their name on the job list. The job was then erased from the board. As we got down to the last jobs on the list, there were always one or two jobs that students didn't want to do. Every year it seemed to be a different job that went in and out of flavor! Since I did the draw randomly, students judged it as being fair. The job only lasted for one month in any event.

The following month, all the jobs were posted back on the board. This time, I went down the list and asked every student if they still wanted their job. The rule is they could keep their job for two consecutive months, then they had to give it up. They could "reapply" for their job after a month passed (that way, no one person could have a monopoly on a particularly appealing job). I had my student secretary erase the jobs or leave them on the board. I removed the names of those students who opted to keep their jobs from my "lottery" container. Once this was done, I randomly picked the remaining names and, as before, I asked students which jobs they would like to do. If there were any jobs left over, I then asked students who would like to take on a second or third job.

By following this procedure, you'll go a long way to building up respect and trust among your students, since you will be respecting and trusting them to do their jobs and accept responsibility in the class.

A quick way to build responsibility and respect for class materials (and a way of not losing them) is to employ this tip I first learned from Barbara Coloroso[54] over thirty-five years ago. I've since added a few twists to it.

When students want to borrow a pair of scissors, a pencil, pen, some masking tape, or other class supply that you want returned, ask them for a shoe in return. At first, they will look at you with a surprised and incredulous expression on their faces. Some refuse. For others who know me from previous years and by reputation, this is not surprising. Taking off one of their shoes to exchange for one borrowed item (or a second shoe if they're borrowing two items) is an established procedure in my class.

It's a Matter of Trust

Here is a wonderful teachable moment on the meaning of trust and responsibility in the working world. I asked the students why I took a shoe. Some would answer that I wanted my item back and I don't want to lose it. Some would say I wanted their shoes!

I then told students about the first time I bought a car. I didn't have enough money to buy the car, so I went to the bank and borrowed the money. I then asked my class, "If I borrow money from the bank and buy a car, who owns the car?"

"You do," they replied.

"No," I replied back.

"The bank owns my car. They have my car as collateral until I repay the loan."

Some of them get it—they took my car (technically, you give the bank a "mortgage" on your car. They take a "lien".)! Depending on the level of students I'm teaching, I would explain to them all about loan payments, interest, and collateral. I explained that if I didn't pay my loan every month, the bank would take back my car. This lesson also leads to a discussion on mortgages.

A lot of students heard about this term around the dinner table, so I explained it to them as clearly as I could. Since I also taught French, I explained the word's origins (i.e. *mort* in mortgage means "death" in French, and *gage* means "a bet" in French. Originally, "mortgage" was a bet with the lender on paying back the loan before your death.).

Throughout the year, I would keep coming back to the concept of trust. I used other authentic examples, such as borrowing money and the use of credit cards. I liked to show students a twenty-dollar bill and ask them what it represented. Then I would tell them that all money is, is trust. People trust it and use it to buy things. I gave examples from my own travels, where the money in the countries where I traveled wasn't trusted by their own citizens. They used American currency, which they trusted instead. I also showed students a credit card. I asked them why I could go into a store/restaurant or get gas, and all I had to do is show a credit card. On top of that, I asked why, on the basis of my signature alone, I didn't have to pay in cash. I explained the entire process.

Then I asked students why they would trust my signature. That's when I would bring up examples of building trust by being responsible for paying my bills each month. I also told them that when I first owned a credit card I had a low credit limit. Only through being responsible and respecting the credit agreement was I able to get a higher credit limit. By respecting my responsibilities, I got more privileges. Students will too, *if* they are responsible.

Field Trips

When your students consistently show respect, responsibility, and trust, you can show them one of the highest forms of responsibility and trust: taking them on a field trip beyond the school.

Field trips can be great learning tools. They reward and motivate your students. Before planning a field trip, read your school and district policies. You will need to know such things as use of permission forms and medical information, criteria for bringing along parents, the required adult-to-student ratio, what to do during an emergency, emergency procedures and phone numbers, and high risk activities, as well as acceptable places to visit.

Review the expectations for student behavior on the field trip. Remind students that they are not only representing themselves, but their school and their parents.

Whether you go on some field trips, such as overnight trips, will depend on the maturity level of your class and the costs involved. Plan overnight trips, depending on where you go and the costs involved, well in advance.

You can choose short trips on shorter notice and with less planning.

The local library is usually my first field trip. Before the trip, I surveyed the class for students who did not have a library card. I made arrangements with the staff for library card applications for said students. For some students, it was their first visit to the library.

Getting the Most out of Field Trips

Field trips are a great way to integrate your curriculum with "real life" learning experiences. One way I did this was to have students take along an exercise book. I had them answer the questions "Who?", "What"? "When?",

"Where?", "Why?" and "How?" Take up the answers in class. It will provide a good debrief of the trip.

Field trips also give you a great opportunity to see how your students behave in situations outside the classroom and school. Field trips are also a learning opportunity. You will learn much about yourself too, especially when things don't go as planned!

Field trips are a great opportunity to get to know those parents who come as volunteers. I would introduce parents and assign a task for my students. Their task was to find out what the parents' interests are, what they did over the summer, or their plans for the weekend.

After the trip, I had students thank the parents with a Pat on the Back. This is a job that I assigned to two of my students. Their job was to trace their hand on a blank piece of paper, color and decorate it. At the top of the page were the words:

"A Pat On The Back to: Mr./Mrs./Ms. for coming on our field trip to_____."

Every student then signed the Pat on the Back. Then I would sign, date the hand, and thank the parent as well. This is an easy way to show your appreciation for the parent's time and participation. It is a model for your students on how to do a proper thank you.

We also thanked our bus and other drivers. Before students left the bus, I publicly thanked the bus driver for safely getting us to the destination. I asked all students to show their appreciation. As students left the bus, they each thanked the bus driver by name. This is another way to model respect for people who do something for you.

It is always a good idea to reinforce your expectations for the field trip before you leave the classroom. Your school and district policies can guide the consequence of misbehavior. Some students, unless they have close supervision, have a difficult time being in an unstructured setting such as a field trip. Other students who have a history of misbehavior on field trips may need to lose the privilege of going altogether. Whether you can hold students back from a trip depends on your school and district policies.

One of the most difficult things I've ever had to do to a class is to cancel our end-of-the-year trip because of misbehavior. I firmly believe that students should earn the right to go on an end-of-the-year field trip. Sometimes students feel entitled. Others automatically assume the class will be going and let their behavior slide. Here is an opportunity to show leadership while making a decision which may not prove too popular.

In twenty-nine years, I had only twice cancelled the end-of-the-year trip. Doing so was emotionally difficult, especially on a hot sunny day at the end of the year when other classes were going on their field trips. However, the decisions sent a very strong message to the next years' students coming into my class: I say what I mean, and I do what I say. It's your integrity and reputation as a teacher that is being defined.

NEXT STEPS:

1. Let students choose their jobs. See the *How to Succeed as an Elementary Teacher Workbook* (found here: http://thebusyeducator.com/succeednow) for a list of jobs. Students who are motivated to take on responsibilities will more than likely do a better job than those who aren't.

2. Use a fair and equitable way to hand out the jobs.

3. Make sure there is a variety of jobs available.

4. Make the jobs important.

5. Train students how to do the job properly.

6. Have students who have done a job train their replacements.

7. See the Field Trip handout in the *How to Succeed as an Elementary Teacher Workbook.*

8. Have students take along an exercise book. Have them answer the questions "Who?", "What?", "When?", "Where?", "Why?" and "How?" Take up the answers in class.

9. Send a Pat on the Back to all field trip volunteers.

Chapter 3:

Smoothing the Foundation

How to Overcome Obstacles

*"The pessimist complains about the wind.
The optimist expects it to change. The leader adjusts the sails."*

John Maxwell

There are many ways to overcome the obstacles you will encounter in teaching your class. One way is to pick the right time. For example, it's never a good time to deal with incidents in the classroom while you are angry. Hold your temper, maintain your cool, bite your tongue, and wait. When you settle down, address any particularly upsetting situations. My old vice principal once told me that when you feel the anger rushing up inside you, that's when you should count to ten.

In a calm, cool, and collected manner, introduce changes the next class day. Doing so gives you time to collect your thoughts and analyze the problem. Sometimes students can be your best asset in times like these. I've often used the entire morning with input from students to work through a problem. The key to finding solutions to classroom problems is not to immediately assign blame. Instead, you can overcome most problems by following this simple model and asking these questions:

- What is the problem? State it in clear, simple language.
- What happened to cause the problem?
- How can we solve it and make the situation better (or what can we do to solve it)?

It's Not the Problem— It's How you Deal with the Problem

One year, I was the school guidance teacher to Grade Seven and Eight students. One day, a substitute teacher, very upset and distraught, left the class I was about to teach. It didn't take long for me to see why. Students were boisterous, rude, and not sitting in their seats. I looked up to see the ceiling tiles perforated with pencils. The students had sharpened them and thrown them into the ceiling tiles over and over again. They did this until they were stuck up there while the substitute teacher was teaching.

When they've been "caught" doing something inappropriate, students usually react in many different ways. One is to deny that they did anything wrong. Another is to blame someone else. Still another way is to remain silent and not say a word.

The first thing I did was tell the students very calmly that I wasn't there to blame anyone. I just wanted to know what happened and how to improve the situation. I used a "round table technique", in which I asked every student for input without judging it. I wanted them all to take part and to give me their versions of the facts. After some discussion, we came up with the problem. The class was disrespectful to the substitute teacher. We then discussed what happened to cause the problem. This time I put on the board the name of every student who wanted to take part. I went through every students' name and put a check mark beside them when the students were finished. When all had their chance to say something, we then discussed how to make the situation better. Again, I used the same system with names on the board. Together the students came up with a solution to the problem.

By listening to the students and modeling respect, I was able to get their cooperation. They respected the process, me, and each other. They could also see the consequences of their actions.

I have used this process very successfully a number of times to deal with teasing, bullying, and fighting in the classroom[55].

NEXT STEPS:

1. Hold your temper, maintain your cool, bite your tongue, and wait.

2. In a calm, cool, and collected manner, introduce changes the next day.

3. You can overcome most problems by following this simple model and asking these questions:

   - What is the problem? State it in clear, simple language.

   - What happened to cause the problem?

   - How can we solve it and make the situation better (or what can we do to solve it)?

Change

Sometimes change is necessary for your class to run smoothly. It may involve a rearrangement of seating, the breaking up of cliques in the class, or a tightening up of the rules, routines, and procedures. Sometimes throughout the year, fatigue sets in. We lose a bit of our motivation and persistence, and start to let some things go. What you permit, you condone. What you condone promotes the behavior that you permitted.

One good exercise to deal with changes is to create a vision for yourself of what your class should look like. Ask yourself, "What kind of class do I want to have?" When the class seems to be slipping, you may ask, "What can I do to move the class to where I want them to be?" This is similar to what pilots do. They make many course changes to account for unexpected weather, wind currents, tailwinds, and traffic to guide the airplane to its destination.

Best Times to Reinforce Change

There are better times than others to reinforce your discipline code, rules, routines, and procedures. When a problem occurs, catch it and change it when it happens. For lining up problems, repeat the process until it's done right. During a physical education class, if there is too much bickering going on, you might cancel the class. You can then debrief with the students then and there what's not going right and how to correct it. You can always do it again in the next physical education period.

For making minor changes, I liked to fine-tune my classroom management on a Monday. On Mondays, I was rested and the class was still fresh from the weekend. I talked to the students first thing in the morning and reinforced what they did well the week before. Then I focused on a procedure they were not doing well. This could've been keeping their desks clean, talking during transition times, or not lining up properly. If I needed to make any major changes or reinforcements, I liked to introduce them after holidays or during natural breaks in the school year, such as between terms or between major teaching units.

After the first term and Christmas break, when students returned for the new year, I liked to start off fresh with New Year's resolutions and a new unit reviewing goal setting.

The New Year—Starting it off Right

The new year is a great time to start fresh, a lot like you did on the first day of school in September. Here's a chance to reinforce your goals for the class, as well as an opportunity to look back to what you and they did well the first term. After all, the word *January* comes from the two-headed Roman god Janus, the god of gates and beginnings. One head looked backwards to the past and the other head looked forwards to the future. You and your class do the same.

Here's how I started the year. As students entered the class, I gave them a sheet of paper to copy the three resolutions I'd written on the front board. This exercise showed the students that the new year is a new beginning. Here is the list I had for the students:

1. What is something we need to do more often?
2. What do we need to improve?
3. What is something we need to stop doing?

When students finished, I filed their sheets into their student folders. Then, before the last term began, I interviewed each student about their resolutions and whether they achieved them.

January is a new beginning, a time for goal setting, for resolving, and for doing your best. Consequently, I spent time doing a goal setting unit based on a movie about Michael Jordan, called *Michael Jordan to the Max*.

I tried to rejuvenate and reenergize over the holidays. In addition to previewing the Michael Jordan movie, I also watched teacher-useful movies. I liked to watch *The Dead Poet's Society*, *The Emperor's Club*, and *12 Angry Men* (to review the twelve different learning styles and personality types, and how to deal with them).

After the spring or March Break, when there is only one term of school left, I liked to review Michael Jordan's quote on failure[56]:

> "I've missed more than 9,000 shots in my career.
>
> I've lost almost 300 games.
>
> 26 times I've been trusted to take the game winning shot and missed.
>
> I've failed over and over again in my life.
>
> And that's why I succeed."

Michael never gives up!

During the longer breaks is also a great time to view and discuss movies such as *Miracle On Ice, Apollo 13, Gandhi, Fly Away Home, The Lord of The Rings: The Fellowship of the Ring, To Kill A Mockingbird, The Karate Kid, Holes, Like Mike, Freaky Friday, Mean Girls, Spiderman, I Like Mike, Tuck Everlasting, Swiss Family Robinson, The Princess Bride, The Dark Crystal,* etc.

At the end of the year, I showed *Back to the Future*. This film shows how events in their past can affect their future. The classic movie *It's A Wonderful Life* also graphically shows a cause-and-effect relationship.

Please Note: Always review any movie you are going to show your class. Some of these movies may not be suitable for lower grades.

Also, be sure you can legally show those films. A classroom showing may be deemed "a public performance" which can usually only be done under a license to do so. Check with your school/district administration for showing of films in which rights have been purchased.

Another subtler way to reinforce your discipline code, rules, routines, procedures, and values all year long is through the use of read-aloud books. I tailored the books that I read out loud to the type of students I had. For many years, I read to my students *The Time Warp Trio* by Jon Scieszka[57]. It is a series that especially appeals to boys and reluctant readers. Through *The Time Warp Trio* books, I could show students the value of having an education, of cooperation, group decision making, tolerance, respect for others, diversity and multiculturalism, and creative problem solving in a fun way without giving them another lecture. The books and themes have now been made into an animated cartoon show.

One of my main goals as a teacher was to teach my students to read. Many of my students were reading below their grade level, some as much as three years! Unfortunately, most of those students were boys.

The following is a wonderful resource to help boys (and girls) with reading: *Me Read? No Way! A Practical Guide to Improving Boys' Literacy Skills.*

http://www.edu.gov.on.ca/eng/document/brochure/meread/index.html

This guide, available for free from the above website, was prepared by the Ontario Ministry of Education as part of an initiative to support student success in literacy. In particular, it focuses on boys' literacy.

This guide offers a rich source of practices and strategies that are being used in successful literacy programs for boys around the world, and that educators can draw on to create a stimulating and engaging learning environment for both boys and girls.

It's a great resource with a lot of great tips. I highly recommend it.

NEXT STEPS:

1. Print out the New Year's Resolutions handout in the *How to Succeed as an Elementary Teacher Workbook* (found here: http://thebusyeducator. com/succeednow)

2. For parent and teacher movie reviews, go to: The Best Teacher in the movies all of time http://www.imdb.com/list/ls053390797/

   Top 12 Must-See Teacher Movies http://www.teachhub.com/top-12-must-see-teacher-movies

   Top Ten Inspirational Teacher Movies https://reelrundown.com/movies/Top-Ten-Teacher-Movies-of-all-Time

3. For children's movies, go to:

   A list of 100 top children's movies (according to The New York Times Essential Library: Children's Movies) for children ages eight to twelve: http://www.filmsite.org/100kidsfilms.html

   Common Sense Media https://www.commonsensemedia.org/

   Kids-in-mind http://www.kids-in-mind.com/

   The Internet Movie Database http://imdb.com/

4. Go to Jim Trelease's website on the importance of read-aloud books and literacy: http://www.trelease-on-reading.com/

How to Unstuck A Class

"What you are is what you have been.
What you'll be is what you do now."

Buddha

"You don't decide your future.
You decide your habits and habits decide your future."

Steve Mehr

There may be times things aren't going quite as well as you'd like. You or your class may feel bogged down, experience low energy, and fall into a rut.

Every road has some ruts. There are many ways to overcome the ruts in your class' learning journey.

Mnemonics

Difficult learning concepts can frustrate learning. I experienced this when I needed to teach long division[58] to my fifth graders. For years I experienced their pain, until I discovered a mnemonic.

A mnemonic is a way to remember a phrase or concept with letters or phrases or images. Well-known mnemonics include the following[59]:

- The order of taxonomy:

Kids Prefer Cheese Over Fried Green Spinach.

(Kingdom, Phylum, Class, Order, Family, Genus, Species).

- Treble clef notes:

The lines on the staff: Every Good Boy Deserves Fudge (E, G, B, D, F).

The spaces on the staff: Furry Animals Cook Excellently (F, A, C, E).

- Bass clef notes:

The lines on the staff: Good Boys Do Fine Always (G, B, D, F, A).

The spaces on the staff: All Cows Eat Grass (A, C, E, G).

- Order of Planets:

119

My Very Excited Mother Just Served Us Nine Pies

(Mercury, Venus, Earth, Mars, Jupiter, Saturn, Uranus, Neptune, and Pluto).

Or without Pluto: My Very Educated Mother Just Served Us Noodles.

- Order of math operations:

Please Excuse My Dear Aunt Sally.

(Parentheses, Exponents, Multiply, Divide, Add, and Subtract).

- The order of the Great Lakes from west to east:

Super Man Helps Every One.

(Superior, Michigan, Huron, Erie, Ontario).

- Names of the Great Lakes:

HOMES.

(Huron, Ontario, Michigan, Erie, Superior).

The first eight U.S. presidents:

Will A Jolly Man Make A Jolly Visitor?

(George Washington, John Quincy Adams, Thomas Jefferson, James Madison, James Monroe, John Quincy Adams, Andrew Jackson, Martin Van Buren).

- The Royal Houses of England and Great Britain:

No Plan Like Yours To Study History Wisely.

(Norman, Plantagenet, Lancaster, York, Tudor, Stuart, Hanover, Windsor).

The seven articles of the United States Constitution:

Large Elephants Jump Slowly And Sink Rapidly.

(Legislative, Executive, Judicial, Supremacy, Amendment, Statehood, Ratification).

The mnemonic I used to teach long division was EDMSB: Every Dead Monkey Smells Bad[60], the five steps in solving a division problem – estimate, divide, multiply, subtract, and bring down.

The key to its success was the presentation. Two days before I had to teach long division, I would casually mention to students that "Every Dead Monkey Smells Bad". I would say it to individual students lined up to come to our class; I would say it before a math lesson; I would write it down in their planners.

The day of the lesson, I made up a poster showing what the mnemonic stood for and a step by step description of the long division steps.

Visual or Kinesthetic Mnemonics[61] [62]

Another effective strategy to help students remember concepts is the use of visual or kinesthetic mnemonics. In mathematics, I've used the following:

To teach a right angle, have students make a right angle with their arm (Have them show their muscle!).

To teach an acute angle, have students make their right-angle arm go towards them, making it smaller.

To teach an obtuse angle, have students make their right-angle arm go away from them.

I also used this technique to help them remember the parts of a newspaper story:

Have students stand.

For the headline, have students touch their head.

For the dateline, have students make a line with their finger.

For the byline, have students wave goodbye.

For the lead, have students lead a horse.

For the body, have students outline a body.

For the ending, have students put two hands behind their hips.

I've used kinesthetics to give students a concrete example of measurement. When discussing the height of Mount Everest, we would go outside to our soccer field and pace one hundred meters. I told them that a climber would have to do that over eighty times straight up to climb to the top of Mount Everest.

If elite performers[63] are using visualization exercises for peak performance, our students should also be using it. Here are just three examples:[64]

> Boxing legend Muhammad Ali was always stressing the importance of seeing himself victorious long before the actual fight.
>
> As a struggling young actor, Jim Carrey used to picture himself being the greatest actor in the world.
>
> Michael Jordan always took the last shot in his mind before he ever took one in real life.

The following are two visualization activities I used with students. For language arts, I had students close their eyes while I read aloud a story to them. I ask them to make pictures or a movie of what I was reading in their heads. This exercise helped them better remember and appreciate our read-aloud novel.

I used a visualization exercise just before math tests. I would turn off the lights, play some calming music, and have students lower their heads on their desks and close their eyes.

I told my students to visualize their last math test:

"Visualize all the mistakes you made. Take an eraser and erase them all. Now, look at your new sheet. Imagine you have every blank filled with an answer. Every answer has a check mark beside it. You look up at the top of the page and you see your name. Beside your name, you see 100 out of 100. Perfect. Excellent. You see yourself getting an I Did It Award for a perfect math test. You take the award home and show your parents. They smile and congratulate you."

If the class had been too noisy and I had a hard time settling them down, I used the same technique this way:

I waited until after recess or lunch to implement this strategy. I turned on soft music, usually for yoga or meditation. It was either the Amazon rainforest or the gentle waves of a beach; relaxing settings. I dimmed the lights or turned them off and had students go to their seats and put their heads down. I told the students, "You're not in trouble. We need to rewind the movie. You just need to relax and calm down before I can teach you." The activity lasts for ten to fifteen minutes. It's an effective way of calming them down and getting the class ready to learn for the next lesson.

I used an extension to this activity to wrap up the week. During my physical education classes, I would use the last ten minutes to do this visualization exercise:

I had students lie on mats, eyes closed. I turned off the lights and reviewed the week. I mentioned the great things that had happened, gave a shout out for some students and staff members. I would mention some things we needed to focus on and get better. I also reviewed some of the activities we would be doing next week. I reminded them of deadlines for projects and what tests to study for. I wished them all a great weekend.

Here's a sample guided listening activity during physical education classes:
> Concentrate on your breathing. Focus on your breaths. Breathe in through your nose and breathe out through your mouth.

Think about the great week you've had. On Monday, you worked together in groups to study polygon definitions. Then you helped each other with the answers to the math sheet and crossword puzzle.

On Tuesday, you walked with your swimming buddy to the pool. They opened the rock wall to climbers and I saw a lot of you encouraging each other to climb to the top. I saw all of you having fun, all of you getting along together.

Then on Wednesday, some of you weren't mutually respecting each other. You weren't being attentive listeners. It was like the Troll Story[65]. However, unlike the Troll Story, many of you were very sorry for what happened. You made it better. You made it right.

Although we all have our differences, we all need to listen to one another, support and help one another. We're like a family. We all share a classroom together. We're all in this together.

Make sure your shoelaces are tied. Be safe. Have a great weekend.

Students were often skeptical when I told them the advantages of visualization. Even after telling them how much my squash game improved after visualization, there were still doubters. That's when I did the following activity[66]:

Have students stand. Tell them, "I want you to put your feet eight to twelve inches apart (twenty to thirty cm.), shoulder-width apart. Make sure you don't have anything in your hands (pens, pencils, notebooks), just put them on your desk. Watch me as I demonstrate. In a moment, I'm going to ask you to put up your right arm. I'm going to use my left arm because I'll be mirroring you. What I'm going to ask you to do is turn across your own body and twist your body as far as you can. When you can't go any further, notice that there is a laser beam pointing off the end of your finger. Remember that spot where your arm couldn't go any further. And so we're going to do that. And then I'm going to show you the power of visualization to improve your ability to perform.

Make sure you don't hit anyone in the head with your arm! Make sure no one is in the way of your turning. I want to make sure your turning stops because you can't turn anymore, not because of an obstacle, like someone's head! Keep your feet glued to the floor. Make sure not to move your feet. Just move your arm and body. That's so you can compare results fairly.

Okay. Right arm up. And go ahead and turn as far as you can and when you can't turn any further, notice where your hand is pointing. And then like a digital camera, take a picture in your mind and memorize what's to the right and what's to the left, and then come back to the middle. Now, just close your eyes for a second and I'm just going to ask you to visualize something two times. I'm just going to ask you to imagine, don't do it, but just imagine that you're lifting your right arm again. Imagine that you're moving it across your body to get to the same spot you went to last time but this time you're able to go a foot or two feet further (thirty to sixty cm.) without any pain or strain. You're just able to go further. Now as you do that, create a new image in your mind where your hand will be pointing. Use the information from your last digital picture; where would it be pointing now? Make that image as clear and as powerful as you can. Some of you will see it clearly, some of you won't. Make it as clear as you can. See it in color if you can. Then imagine bringing your arm back to the middle and down to your side. Your eyes are still closed. And just imagine that one more time. Imagine lifting up your right arm, moving it across your body, going to that first spot, then going one to two feet further to the second spot; notice what it looks like and get a clear picture of it. Use the power of your creative mind. Okay, bring your arm back to the middle and down to your side. Open your eyes. This is what we're going to do. We're going to lift up our arm again and go one more time, and go as far as we can; see how far we can go. Let's see what happens. Here we go. Come back to the middle. How many of you went further by show of hands? Very good. Take a seat."

What this exercise shows that if we visualize a result, our body can produce it. Every time I did this with a class, friends, relatives, or by myself, I got the same result. Try it for yourself. Then try it with your class.

Here's a mnemonic to show students how to listen to a speaker:

S   Sit up.

L   Listen.

A   Ask and answer questions.

N   Nod your head.

T   Track the speaker.

Put this on a poster and review it with your class until it becomes a habit.

Teamwork

If students are bickering about working in teams, you may want to show your class this example:

A conductor of a symphony wanted to show his audience the team concept. As the symphony started to play, he started to remove musicians and instruments one by one, until there was none left. He told the audience that every musician and instrument is important to the orchestra. Great music can only be played by all the members.

An extension of this in the classroom can be shown in physical education classes. During basketball, baseball, volleyball, or any team sport, remove a player from one team until there is only one player left. One person is never better than the rest of the team.

Listening To Directions

One year I had a very difficult class. Towards the end of the year, I was getting more and more frustrated trying to get the class to follow my directions. It was a battle which I was losing, and the class knew it. I was beside myself not knowing what to do.

My colleague told me of a book[67] he was reading with some different techniques. I was skeptical that such an easy-to-use technique would work with such a tough class. I tried it. My mouth dropped when I saw it working with my most combative student.

I first used it as students were coming into class after recess. Some of them were talking to their friends and taking their time going to their desks. That's when I used this technique by saying, "I need you all to go to your desks. Great. I need five. I need four. Now I need three. I still need three. I need two. I still need two. Now I need one. We're almost there. Thank you. Let's get started."

I was amazed. It proved to be a life saver in the final weeks of school that year.

Following Directions

This is an activity I first did in Grade Nine. It was a fun way to reinforce the following of directions.

NAME _____ SCORE _____

CAN YOU FOLLOW DIRECTIONS?[68]

1. Read everything carefully before doing anything.

2. Put your name in the upper right-hand corner of this page.

3. Circle the word NAME in sentence two.

4. Draw five small squares in the upper left-hand corner.

5. Put an "X" in each square.

6. Put a circle around each square.

7. Sign your name under the title of this paper.

8. After the title, write "yes, yes, yes."

9. Put a circle completely around sentence number seven.

10. Put an "X" in the lower left corner of this paper.

11. Draw a triangle around the "X" you just put down.

12. On the back of this paper, multiply 703 by 66.

13. Draw a rectangle around the word "corner" in sentence four.

14. Loudly call out your first name when you get this far along.

15. If you have followed directions carefully to this point, call out, "I have."

16. On the reverse side of this paper, add 8950 and 9305.

17. Put a circle around your answer and put a square around the circle.

18. Punch three small holes in the top of this paper with your pencil point.

19. If you are the first person to reach this point, LOUDLY call out, I AM THE FIRST PERSON TO REACH THIS POINT, AND I AM THE LEADER IN FOLLOWING DIRECTIONS."

20. Underline all even numbers on the left side of this paper.

21. Loudly call out, "I AM NEARLY FINISHED. I HAVE FOLLOWED DIRECTIONS."

22. Now that you have finished reading everything, ignore everything except this and the first two sentences.

Igniting Curiosity

Take an object and wrap it up in a box. It can be a small jewelry box or a shoebox. Have one student ask one question a day (for example, is it an animal, vegetable or mineral?). Although this activity takes up little time, students will look forward to it every day until the riddle of the box is solved.[69]

Self-Control

Some of my students had little self-control. When something happened to them, they assumed that it was done on purpose. For example, when pushed from behind in line, they would turn around and hit the other student. I asked them, if it was a grandmother who was behind them, would they hit her? They said "no". I asked why. We discussed the reasons. Then we talked about maybe the student that pushed you tripped, or was pushed from behind themselves.

One of the most effective ways I've used for discussing points of view and looking at all sides of an argument or situation employs a defective soda can (I've also used an empty donut box, a resealed empty box from a popular candy-like cereal, etc.). The can looked like a full can of soda, but it was really empty. The tab was still in place and there were no holes. I showed the students the can and asked them to describe what it is. After the discussion, I lightly tossed the can to a student. The student quickly realized that it was empty. I told the students not to judge anyone until they had all the facts. Don't assume you know everything about a situation until you have all the facts.

Changing Attitudes One Word, One Thought at a Time

I had a poster in my class with a picture of Yoda from the movie *The Empire Strikes Back*. Underneath Yoda is this quote:

"No! Try not. Do or do not. There is no try."

Most students know the quote. I explain the meaning of this quote by doing this activity:

- Put a sheet of paper on the floor.
- Ask a student to try to pick it up.

127

- When a student picks up the paper, stop the student and say "I want you to try and pick it up."

Students quickly realize that there is no try. It is just do.

I did this activity to improve the self-talk[70] attitudes and perspectives in class. It ties in with the themes of overcoming obstacles and goal achievement.

Although this exercise is for students, it was also for me, the teacher. It was a gentle reminder for me to examine my self-talk, my attitudes, and perspectives when teaching. It's important to do during good times, but especially during those frustrating times.

To illustrate how to improve our self-talk is to overcoming obstacles and goal achievement, I've taught the following lesson. It is based on the story "Rest in Peace: The 'I Can't' Funeral", written by teacher Chick Moorman[71] for the first *Chicken Soup for the Soul*™ book[72]. It has now been updated with a lesson plan, student activities, and tips in *The Chicken Soup for the Soul in the Classroom Middle School Edition: Grades 6-8*[73].

I would hand out a piece of paper to students and tell them to write down all the things they "can't" do. We would do this for ten minutes or so, including me.

I took all the papers and put them into a galvanized pail. We went into the schoolyard field and we cremated the excuses. I read this as part of our funeral ceremony: "Boys and girls, please join hands and bow your heads.

"Friends, we gather today to honor the memory of 'I Can't'. While he was with us on earth, he touched the lives of everyone, some more than others. His name, unfortunately, has been spoken in every public building: schools, city halls, state capitals, and yes, even on Capitol Hill.

"We have provided 'I Can't' with a final resting place. He is survived by his brothers and sister 'I Can', 'I Will', and 'I'm Going to Do it Right Away.' They are not as well-known as their famous relative and are certainly not as strong and powerful yet. Perhaps someday, with your help, they will make an even bigger mark on the world.

"May 'I Can't' rest in peace and may everyone present pick up their lives and move forward in his absence. Amen.|

Later, we went back to class have a wake with cake and ice cream. I had a student draw a tombstone with the date when we buried our "I Cant's". When students told me they can't do something, I pointed to the poster and reminded students that we buried our "I Cant's". Most days, I found myself looking at that tombstone poster and reminding myself some of my own "I Cant's".

Instead of going outside to cremate your "I Can't" ashes, you could put them through a shredder. Then put them in a clear container under a R.I.P. sign as a class reminder of their former "I Cant's".

I Can't Poster and Ashes in Our Fifth Grade Class
(Photo by Marjan Glavac)

An extension for this lesson can be found by watching "No Legs, No Arms, No Worries!",[74] a video of Nick Vujicic[75] (there is also a sample lesson plan).

Imagine being born without arms. No arms to wrap around someone, no hands to experience touch, or to hold another hand with. Or what about being born without legs? Having no ability to dance, walk, run, or even stand on two feet? Now put both of those scenarios together – no arms and no legs. What would you do? How would that effect your everyday life? This is Nick Vujicic's story.

(Please note: You should supervise these plans for appropriateness depending on your class, administration, and parents.)

An extension to this lesson is to have students write on a piece of paper all the things they *can* do. Collect these and put them into their personal files. Have students review them on a regular basis. You can also post them as a class reminder of the things they can do beside the I Did It poster below:

I capped this lesson on changing attitudes one word, one thought at a time with this quote[76] from Mahatma Ghandi:

"Keep your thoughts positive, because your thoughts become your words.
Keep your words positive, because your words become your behavior.
Keep your behavior positive, because your behavior become your habits.
Keep your habits positive, because your habits become your values.
Keep your values positive, because your values become your destiny."
Open Your Mind, Open Your Life: A Book of Eastern Wisdom

Zingers

To change the pace and to make lessons more interesting in class, I would occasionally add a "zinger". A zinger becomes something special. It involves something unexpected. The surprise breaks a routine. For example, I'd ask the class to turn to a page in their textbook and read quietly for five minutes. Then I would ask them to close their books and tell me something: what was the first word on the page? What was the title? What are three facts from the page you were reading? The first few times, students had difficulty answering the questions. I used these teachable moments to reinforce the question words Who, What, When, Where, Why and How. It also reinforces concentration and focusing skills.

To encourage realism into their writing, I assigned students a daily journal topic. One such topic was, "What would you do if a horse were to come galloping into the cafeteria during lunch? Describe how you would feel." I'd let students respond to this for a couple of minutes. Then I told them that I was going to demonstrate by being the horse. I instructed everyone to act as if they were eating their lunches or talking to their friends in the cafeteria. Then I turned off the lights, and in the pitch blackness, the only thing the students could hear is the neighing of a horse. I turned on the lights. Once the screams and laughter have subsided, I then told them to write down what they felt like in the dark with a horse coming out of nowhere[77].

To reinforce students putting their names on their assignments, I collected their papers and then put them into a shopping bag. Every time I pulled out an assignment with a name on it, I gave a point to the class or I handed out a lollipop. This, I found, was an excellent reinforcement with tangible rewards, and fun to do.

Sometimes I would do a mock fire drill to see how students responded to the fire drill procedure. The drill is a very good way to practice the procedure, and it's a change of pace to the classroom.

Reasons to Study a Subject[78 79 80 81 82]

French was a hard subject to teach. Students need reasons for learning, especially something difficult like a new language. Here are two strategies I used which you can adapt to other subjects.

Top Ten Reasons to Learn French:

10. To be able to communicate with someone when you are in France or Quebec, and even parts of Africa, Asia, and the Middle East. More than 220 million people in the world speak French[83].

9. To communicate with French speakers without ever leaving Canada.

8. To improve your English skills.

7. To learn a language for travel. France is the world's top tourist destination and attracts more than 79.5 million visitors a year. Paris is one of the most beautiful cities in the world[84].

6. To increase your career opportunities.

5. To learn about French places, music, movies, theatre, fashion, dance, and literature.

4. To learn about French history.

3. To learn to appreciate (and order) wonderful French foods.

2. It helps sharpen your mind.

1. It makes you an interesting person.

I make a connection with something they already know to show them how easy it is:

"So you think French is hard!"

I take it you already know
Of tough and bough and cough and dough.
Others may stumble, but not you,
On hiccough, thorough, though, and through -
Well done!
And now you wish perhaps
To learn of less familiar traps?
Beware of heard, a dreadful word
That looks like beard and sounds like bird,
And dead - it's said like bed, not bead.
Watch out for meat and great and threat
(They rhyme with suite and straight and debt).
A moth is not a moth in mother,
Nor both in bother, broth in brother.
And here is not a match for there
Nor dear and fear for bear and pear.
And then there's dose and rose and lose,
Just look them up — goose and choose
And cork and work and card and ward
And front and font, and word and sword
And do and go, and wart and cart -
Come! Come! I've hardly made a start!
A dreadful language? Man alive!
I mastered it — when I was five!!!

– Author unknown

133

What to Do When You are Finished

I had this poster in my class to remind students what they could do when they are finished:

MATH

- Memorize math facts $+ - \times \div$
- Review math concepts and formulas.

LANGUAGE ARTS

- Read quietly.
- Write a story.
- Memorize difficult spelling words.

CATCH UP

- Homework assignments.
- Study for upcoming tests.

FRENCH

- Memorize "chaise chaud" questions and answers.

ORGANIZE

- Your folders, binders, desk.

Tempus Fugit—Time Flies

Throughout the first month, I would secretly time how long students took to settle down to a task in class and to line up before school, after morning recess, at lunch, and afternoon recess. I did this once or twice a week for about a month to get a baseline. By the second month, times usually increased. I then taught students the power of increments. If we wasted ten minutes a day for one hundred days, we lost one thousand minutes. One thousand minutes equals a little over sixteen hours - over two days of teaching! These are days that we could've been swimming or taking a field trip, for example. I also told them the times we wasted during transitions and going to rotary classes. When students first become aware of time in this way, they also start to assume more responsibility for their actions. I used the same technique to teach students the cost of smoking over twenty, thirty, and forty years. I sometimes asked, "How would you like to get a free house?" Then I showed them how a two pack-a-day smoker could buy one with the money they burned by their smoking.

More Zinger Boredom Busters

Another way to get unstuck is to use the following Zinger Boredom Busters:
- Humor: Telling corny jokes.
- Toboggan on a nearby hill.
- Swim.
- Skate.
- Play soccer ball in the snow.
- Play broomball in the snow.
- Design an "unbreakable" box for eggs and then test them by dropping each one from the top of the school.
- Play balloon volleyball in class.
- Give students a personal activity time.
- Hold draws/auctions.
- Have an impromptu recess—stay outside/dismiss class early and go outside with you supervising them.
- Have a bubblegum chewing contest.
- Enjoy class parties for Halloween, Christmas, and at the end of the term.
- Hold special days: Hat Day, Christmas in June day, a Beach Day in February, etc.
- Have a Paper Airplane Flying Contest.
- During physical education class, have teams wrap up one person like a mummy using toilet paper (ties in perfectly with an Egyptian unit).
- Play Twenty Questions.
- Hold a Spelling Bee.
- Teach students how to play chess.

Boredom Zingers for Specific Classes:
- Art – one teacher I knew had students tape a blank sheet of art paper under their desks. Then he had the students lie on their backs and draw

135

on the art paper. He told them this is how Michelangelo painted the Sistine Chapel.[85]

- Math – have students pair up and complete The Metric Me handout See the *How to Succeed as an Elementary Teacher Workbook* (found here: http://thebusyeducator.com/succeednow).
- Review the curriculum through games such as Trivial Pursuit®, Who Wants To Be A Millionaire ™, Wheel of Fortune®, Survivor®, etc.

Using Camp Songs to Motivate

One year I took my class to the auditorium stage in our gymnasium. I brought in my Christmas lights, formed them in a circle, and plugged them in to make an imaginary camp fire. I taught the students the following songs[86]:

The Princess Pat

The leader sings one line, others repeat; actions are in brackets.

The Princess Pat (Egyptian pose)

Light infantry (salute)

They sailed across (wave motion in front of body with one hand)

The seven seas (number seven with your finger, then make a "C" with one hand)

They sailed across (wave motion)

The channel two (two hands tracing a channel, then number 2 on one hand)

And took with them (throw a sack over your shoulder)

A rick-a-bamboo! (trace a wavy figure in front of you going down, bend knees as you go)

A rick-a-bamboo (same as before)

Now what is that? (shrug shoulders, hold out hands)

It's something made (bang one fist on top of the other)

For the Princess Pat (Egyptian pose)

It's red and gold ("twirl" one arm down by your hip)

And purple too (flip hands as if you were saying "Oh my gosh!")

That's why it's called (cup hands in front of mouth, shout)

A rick-a-bamboo! (same as before)

Now Captain Dan (salute)

And his loyal crew (salute several times)

They sailed across (wave action)

The channel two (same as before)

But their ship sank (plug nose, one hand over head and waving as you bend knees)

And yours will too (point to others in the circle)

Unless you take (throw an invisible bag over your shoulder)

A rick-a-bamboo! (same as before)

A rick-a-bamboo (same as before)

Now what is that? (shrug shoulders, hold out hands)

It's something made (bang one fist on top of the other)

For the Princess Pat (Egyptian pose)

It's red and gold ("twirl" one arm down by your hip)

And purple too (flip hands as if you were saying "Oh my gosh!")

That's why it's called (cup hands in front of mouth, shout)

(everyone together) A rick-a-bamboo! (same as before)

The following links will provide the tune for "The Princess Pat", as well as some additional verses to the song.

https://www.youtube.com/watch?v=ARMEmFPYUK4

https://www.youtube.com/watch?v=UQ6G-kUHUqE

https://www.youtube.com/watch?v=6i35hm_-NXw

https://www.youtube.com/watch?v=lmCsBNYK6T4

Bob and Tom — Toast

All around the country, coast to coast,

People always say, what do you like most,

I don't wanna brag, I don't wanna boast,

I always tell 'em, I like toast.

Yeah TOAST! Yeah TOAST!

I get up in the mornin', bout six AM,

Have a little jelly, have a little jam,

Take a piece of bread, put it in the slot,

Push down the lever and the wires gets hot,

I get toast.

Yeah TOAST! Yeah TOAST!

Now there's no secret to toasting perfection,

There's a dial on the side and you make your selection,

Push to the dark or the light and then,

If it pops too soon press down again,

Make toast.

Yeah TOAST! Yeah TOAST!

When the first caveman drove in from the drags,

Didn't know what would go with the bacon and the eggs,

Must have been a genius got it in his head,

Plug the toaster in the wall,

Buy a bag of bread,

Make toast.

Yeah TOAST! Yeah TOAST!

Oui monsieur, bonjour croquette,

Uh huh croissante vous a ver,

Maurice Chevalier Eiffel Tower,

Oh oui Maria baguette bonsoir,

FRENCH TOAST! FRENCH TOAST!

YEAH TOAST!

https://www.youtube.com/watch?v=SHptn_3RyYE

https://www.youtube.com/watch?v=uVrm5bZgqcg

I also brought in small sticks from an apple tree in my backyard and a bag of marshmallows. We "roasted" the marshmallows on our imaginary camp fire. After singing the songs and "roasting" our marshmallows, the mood in the class really changed after that.

And Sometimes, You Have to tell it Like it Is

There are things you can let go in the classroom, and there are things that you have to address.

This is a talk I gave to my class early in the school year. I had them all sit in community circle.

> First of all, let me say that I love all of you very, very much. I believe in you, I know you can handle it, I accept all of you. I want all of you in our classroom.
>
> On the very first day of school, I made a promise to each and every one of you that this would be your best year ever. In order to keep that promise, I need something from you: I need you to do your best, to follow the rules of the classroom, to respect yourself and each other, to be responsible for your actions, to co-operate; to be a TEAM.
>
> I've always believed that students should know where they are, where they're going, and how to get there.
>
> I'm not going to hold anything back. You all failed your math test.
>
> It's feedback you may not want to hear, but the reason you all failed is because your behavior is impacting your academic work. There's a number of things you've forgotten or haven't learned.
>
> And that's my job, to help you be your best. I'm phoning all your parents. They need to know. We're going to re-do the test. I'll show you how to answer the questions today.
>
> You need to start taking home your math every night and reading out loud the questions, reviewing what we did in class, and giving me feedback the next day on what confused you.
>
> You need to start talking to each other – by phone, text, or in-person – helping each other, supporting each other.
>
> It's through education that I got out of poverty, my brother got out of poverty, my sister got out of poverty. It's the reason why my kids don't live in poverty. That's one of my biggest values, and our society's values – that's why education is free for everyone from K to Grade Twelve. I want you to do your best, your parents want you to do your best.
>
> Now we need you to do your best.

When Nothing Works

There comes a time when none of your work, preparation, incentives, awards, zinger boredom busters, routines, rules, procedures, or speeches are as effective as they once were. Students won't perform as well as they once did. Their motivation and morale will be low and you will feel frustrated. At that point, your class is truly stuck. Here's an activity that will help you get your class unstuck.

How to Take Control in Your Classroom and Put an End to Constant Fights and Arguments

My old principal often told us at our staff meetings that the reputation of our school was "blood and guts". It was true. The students were tough. Many of the parents were single mothers trying to make a living. Housing was often overcrowded and there was a high incidence of crime. On standard tests, the school consistently scored below the district and provincial average.

There was one year I taught at the school where the students were rude and disrespectful. They were fighting among themselves, constantly bickering and bullying others. There were moments when I stood in front of the entire class, watching helplessly while all this misbehavior was going on.

It was a horrible, depressing feeling. Every morning before school started, I would head off to work with a pit in my stomach.

I didn't want to be there.

I didn't want to face them.

I was getting frustrated and stressed out.

But I had one untried strategy left. Although it would take away time from my curriculum and my goal of increasing class test scores, I had nothing to lose. When used the correct way, this strategy works. If not used correctly, it can backfire on you.

This strategy is very effective when you're tired, frustrated, and stressed out. I used it when I'd exhausted all my bag of tricks. This is not to say that you should never use your other strategies. If the strategy you used didn't work, it could be the class, it could be the timing, or it could be the environment. Its failure could be due to many factors. Put that strategy back into your toolkit and use it again later in the year or with another class.

This easy-to-use strategy to take control in your classroom is the class meeting.

Here's how it works:

The key is in preparation. You will have a minimum of three meetings. One week before your meeting is the time to build up support and anticipation.

Your first meeting is to talk to your key student leaders. Include both boys and girls that you have a good relationship with. If possible, enlist the support of one or more of your "top dogs".

If you need more support, ask a trusted colleague, an administrator, or a consultant from your district to attend the pre-meetings and the actual meeting.

Food is a great motivator. Prepare this ahead of time as one of your lessons (I would often make crepes in my French classes or hummus during one of my lessons on Egypt and the Middle East). Fresh fruit and dessert are also great motivators. Use the food as a reward for the end of the meeting. It becomes a distraction if students are eating during the meeting.

You need to have an agenda that focuses in on exactly what you want to do.

Here's what you want to do in your first pre-meeting with your key students and in your second meeting with the entire class.

You want to keep it simple and ask the following three questions:

- What do you like about our class?
- What's not working in our class?
- How do we make our class better?

Ask the student leaders to give the class their suggestions as examples to get the discussion going. Listen to the suggestions without interrupting. When you believe students understand what to do, hand out a piece of paper for them to write down their thoughts.

Make sure students put their name on their papers. This makes them more accountable for their suggestions. Asking questions and listening for the answers can "unstuck" a class. Are your students overwhelmed with the curriculum, work load, or your expectations? Have they been given enough time to complete their work? Are other rotary teachers giving them major projects and assignments at the same time as you do?

Collect their suggestions. I read all my students' responses as soon as possible, then I reported back to them. Together, we then brainstormed solutions to the problems. You'll be surprised how in tune the children are to the workings of the class and how to get unstuck.

You don't want to lose the momentum. Take the best suggestions and make posters out of them. Present them at your third meeting, preferably the next day. Hang them up in the class. Refer to them as often as necessary.

If the class is starting to feel out of control, point to the posters. Refer to them as often as possible.

At your third meeting, you can personalize and praise suggestions from students (ask students before the meeting if they would like to be acknowledged. Some students may not want to be recognized.). If possible, use suggestions from one of your tougher students.

Why it works:

- This strategy engages and empowers all students.
- It gives all students an equal opportunity to voice their opinions in a very safe environment.
- Shows students that they can make a difference.
- Shows students a practical method on how to solve problems in an orderly way.
- Gives students ownership of their class.
- Demonstrates to students that you listen and are able to act positively without yelling.
- You've shown your students that you respect their decisions.
- In turn, they will respect you.

Don't forget to thank your class after the session with a Pat on the Back.

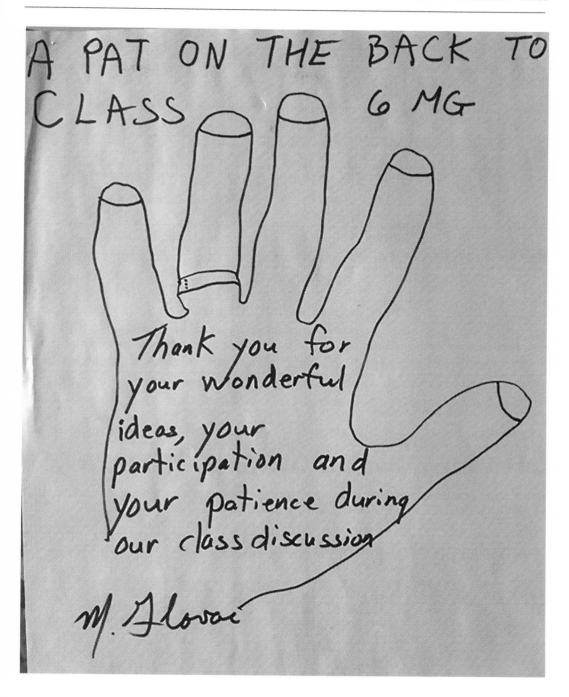

Summary of Main Steps

1. Enlist support of key student leaders, a trusted colleague, and/or an administrator.
2. Keep it simple and ask the three key questions.
3. Listen to suggestions without interrupting.
4. Take the best suggestions and make posters out of them.
5. Present the posters at your third meeting, preferably the next day. Hang them up in the class. Refer to them as often as necessary.

NEXT STEPS:

1. To make difficult concepts easier to learn, use mnemonics.
2. Use visualization techniques with goal setting.
3. To change attitudes, teach the *I Can't* lesson and its extensions.
4. Use a "zinger" to bust boredom in your lessons.
5. When nothing works, teach the lesson on *How to Take Control in Your Classroom and Put an End to Constant Fights and Arguments*.

How to Get Yourself Unstuck

"Hard work, of course, is critical. But you have to balance
that with time for your family and friends.
One-dimensional people are rarely successful over the long haul."

G. Richard Thoman

"If you keep fighting with yourself, you will always win."

Samer Chidiac

There are times when you feel overwhelmed and burned out by all the demands of teaching. It doesn't matter how many long hours you spend, you cannot get ahead. You are irritable with your students, staff, and spouse.

D.H. Lawrence, a teacher before he became a writer, wrote this poem. He describes a teacher who has lost his desire to teach. If many of your teacher days are like this, then there are things that you need to unstuck yourself.

Last Lesson of the Afternoon[87]

D.H. Lawrence

When will the bell ring, and end this weariness?
How long have they tugged the leash, and strained apart,
My pack of unruly hounds! I cannot start
Them again on a quarry of knowledge they hate to hunt,
I can haul them and urge them no more.

No longer now can I endure the brunt
Of the books that lie out on the desks; a full threescore
Of several insults of blotted pages, and scrawl
Of slovenly work that they have offered me.
I am sick, and what on earth is the good of it all?
What good to them or me, I cannot see!

> So, shall I take
> My last dear fuel of life to heap on my soul
> And kindle my will to a flame that shall consume
> Their dross of indifference; and take the toll
> Of their insults in punishment? — I will not! -
>
> I will not waste my soul and my strength for this.
> What do I care for all that they do amiss!
> What is the point of this teaching of mine, and of this
> Learning of theirs? It all goes down the same abyss.
>
> What does it matter to me, if they can write
> A description of a dog, or if they can't?
> What is the point? To us both, it is all my aunt!
> And yet I'm supposed to care, with all my might.
>
> I do not, and will not; they won't and they don't; and that's all!
> I shall keep my strength for myself; they can keep theirs as well.
> Why should we beat our heads against the wall
> Of each other? I shall sit and wait for the bell.

My school psychologist referred to stress as the "silent killer". The first time in my career where I dealt with this silent killer was in my third year of teaching.

I am a very punctual person. Being on time was drilled early into me by parents, school, church, and jobs. I highly value being on time.

In my third year of teaching, I slept in. I had fifteen minutes to get to school.

It bothered me, but not that much. It was a bit out of the ordinary, but nothing to worry about. Or so I thought.

The next day, it was *deja vu* all over again. I slept in again. I got up at the same exact time. I had fifteen minutes to get to school.

This was a sign that I needed a change in my teaching assignment. Things weren't working out in my new school. My principal agreed and arranged a mutual transfer with another teacher.

There are times when every teacher feels some signs of stress. You are tired and exhausted. You're having difficulties making decisions. Sometimes your mind may go blank. You may feel anxious and nervous. You're irritable, impatient, and short tempered with your students. All your bag of tricks and experience can't seem to motivate your students anymore. All you want to do is to wait for the bell. D.H. Lawrence makes the valid point that you can't use up all your strength on your students. Otherwise, you will grow to dislike them all.

One of the most common factors in work-related stress is the lack of control. The more we feel out of control due to unruly students, demands of administrators, and the increased work load, the more we're going to feel stress. There are some things that are out of your control. You can't take any action. There are times when the best approach is to take no action at all. Just let it go. When you don't have control, ask yourself if this battle is worth fighting. Sometimes you'll win the battle, but the resentment will linger. If it's not a "matter of life and death", then you will be fighting a guerilla war all year long.

Stay focused on what you can control. Focus on what you have. Focus on the changes you can make in your own life. This is one of the findings from more than eighty years the Harvard Study of Adult Development has been studying adult life: nearly 70 percent of those who remain healthy and happy in their own age "stay focused on those things they could change in their lives and keep adversities in perspective."[88] [89]

Movie Motivation[90]

At such times, I particularly liked to watch teacher movies. Although *Blackboard Jungle* was made in 1955, it still has important lessons for teachers. Glenn Ford plays the central character. He shows what a teacher can and can't control, how to make incremental changes, and how to savor the small victories while changing student behavior.

I also liked *The Twilight Zone* episode "The Changing of the Guard" (season three, episode thirty-seven; originally aired June 1, 1962).

I was just six years old when I first saw the original airing of this episode from *The Twilight Zone* (long before I had any thoughts of becoming a teacher!). For some reason, years ago I started to think about this episode. I especially remembered the ending:

Professor Ellis Fowler is a teacher who has taught for fifty-one years. The board of trustees has sent him a letter of retirement. He contemplates his teaching career and comes to the conclusion that everything he has taught was a waste. That is, until he enters "The Twilight Zone". In this episode, Rod Serling, the creator of The Twilight Zone, really knew what teachers strive for in their careers. Decades later, it still holds true today.

A more recent movie, *The Emperor's Club* with Kevin Kline, showed me that although I can try my best and do all I can for my students, I can't "fix" them all. There will be failures, especially with students whom I tried to reach, but for whom I was unable to change their behavior. There will be students you can't stop, for whatever reason, from going down the wrong path. This movie shows that for every student you can't change, there will be hundreds of students where you will make a difference. Those you will inspire to do their best through all the little things you do with them all year long. Even though they don't tell you or acknowledge the impact you have on them, in later years they will remember and be grateful for the things you did. Talk to older teachers about the students who came back, the students who went on to make an impact in their communities, the students they remember, and who loved you. You'll have students like these, too.

Here are two examples:

I intervened on behalf of a female student in my class whose brother bullied her relentlessly. Five years later, I learned that the brother was my teenage son's best friend, a person who stood by him when he was bullied.

I tirelessly promoted the importance of reading over and over again to a ten-year-old student who refused to read. Five years later, my nonreader walked into my class and showed me the trilogy of fantasy books that he was proudly reading. He thanked me for turning him on to reading, and handed me a book to read.

I've seen the impact other teachers have had on other peoples' lives. Some time ago in a small rural community, I was attending the funeral of my sister-in-law's father. As I was waiting in line at the funeral home, there were a lot of people who got out of the line to shake the hand of a gentleman in front of me. I told my wife that it must be the mayor of the town since so many people knew him and greeted him by name. I asked my sister-in-law, "Who is that gentleman?" She told me it was a retired Grade Six teacher!

But when it comes to your state of mind, it is critically important that you take time for yourself. For years, I drove to school passing a river that meandered slowly down the middle of the city. In the morning, I'd notice the mist rising from the water and the bright sunshine reflecting off it. Every time I saw this idyllic scene, I regretted going to school. Every day on the way home, I passed the same scene. Then an idea dawned on me: Why not stop and take a few minutes on a picnic bench and admire this scene before I take my stressed-out mind into the house? Now, I find this a great way to unwind from a stressful day. I have the last of the coffee from my thermos or a piece of fruit from my lunch. I sit on a bench and admire the river, the rowers, the kayakers, the birds, and the bicyclists and joggers. I let all the cares of the day melt away before I go home.[91]

Quench the Flames of Burnout

A good exercise to regain your passion and your confidence is to review the "Know Thyself" chapter and survey in the *How to Succeed as an Elementary Teacher Workbook*

(found here: *http://thebusyeducator.com/succeednow*).

As you look it over, ask yourself these questions:

- What was my greatest accomplishment in my career so far?
- What do you really love about teaching?
- What accomplishments am I proud of this year?
- What was the toughest situation I had to deal with? How did I overcome it?

Refocus on what you like about teaching. Draw confidence from your past successes. Let them form positive images in your mind.[92]

When my vice principal would have a bad day, she would phone the parents of her good students. She would let them know what a privilege it was to teach their child. I would look over positive letters from parents. I would also read the positive feedback students and parents wrote on the report card response form. I would also read my Pat on the Backs.

Reading comments like these restored my confidence when I was in a rut:

"We are very pleased with Brittany's report card. It is obvious to us that your dedication to teaching has inspired Brittany's extra effort. Thank–you."

"Melissa has had a wonderful year so far in Grade Five and we hope this continues in the final term. Thank you for your continued support and guidance."

"Mr. Glavac, you seem to have 'turned on' a learning switch in Brittany. Thank you."

"Thank you, Mr. Glavac, for continuing to make this year very informative, interesting, diversified and fun for the students. You are held in high esteem. And we thank you for all your hard work, dedication, and patience."

Celebrate your small victories. My school secretary often saw my one student every day in the office. He was always late, disheveled, lethargic, with his shoes untied. I spent time noticing him and talking to him every day. One day my school secretary was astonished to see his hair combed and shoes tied. He was smiling and interacting with the office staff.

My toughest student was known as a "gangster rapper". He was the first to give me a Christmas card with a CD of Christmas songs.

Another tough student waited the last day of school until all the other students had left the class. He then asked if he could get a hug from me.

Sometimes things seem worse than they actually are. One year I was convinced that I had the worst class of my career, but one day I came to class and all my students were dressed up with a tie, just like me.

Another year, I was again convinced that I had the worst class of my career. It was the year my dad died of a stroke. That year, my class raised the most money of the entire school for the Heart and Stroke Skip-A-Thon fundraiser.

And out of the mouth of babes, this end-of-the-year comment from one of my students:

"I like how Mr. Glavac helps us outa lot. I like how you Did gotcha draws in The class. I like what we do in gym with line soccer and dodgeball. I like how Mr. Glavac encourages us to [do] things that some of us couldn't do at the Beginning of the year. MR. GLAVAC IS The BEST teacher ever! The best!"

The latest research on teacher burnout shows that teachers who are least likely to burn out are those who discuss positive aspects of the job with other teachers. They also associate pleasant emotions with the job. Have a trusted colleague that you can talk about the positives of teaching when you're feeling down.

The Three S's of Stress Relief

Before you can help/support anyone and "fill up their buckets", you need to fill up your own buckets and have your own support mechanisms.

The support mechanism I use is sex, scotch, and salad.[93]

The sex part is your significant other, your partner who there to support you in good times and bad.

The scotch part is for getting away from it all, forgetting the cares of the day through a good drink, a good bottle of wine to be shared with family and friends, or a vacation to recharge your batteries.

The salad part is for eating healthy and getting plenty of exercise.

Only then was I able to support my students the way every effective teacher supports them. I looked for unique strengths, talents, or interests and built on them. I also supported the underdog and the needy student by modifying the curriculum or by throwing it out. I made contact with each and every student at the door to read their mood and help them before they came into the classroom. I showed them how to reach their goals through incremental changes and following up their successes with Sunshine Calls to their parents, personal notes, and face-to-face conversations.

And if I failed, I knew that I gave it my best effort and I knew that there would be another teacher to pick up where I left off.

Here are some other things you can do to deal with burnout and stress[94]: (Just be sure more work doesn't add more stress)

- Have a coffee with a good friend.
- Go out for lunch with some friends.
- Pick something to do just for you.
- Change it up: take a different way to work, eat in a different place, and/or connect with staff members on non-related school topics.

- Set boundaries between your family life and your school life.
- Take on a new task, such as a school or district committee.
- Enroll in a fun workshop, seminar, or conference or personal, non-teaching interest.
- Change your goals.
- Change teaching grade assignments in the school.
- Change schools. A wise principal once asked me, "Would you rather go to a school five minutes away where you're unhappy, or would you rather travel an hour to a school where you're happy?"
- Go into a different teaching role, such as resource or administration.
- Avoid the negative attitude of your colleagues. Be more positive.
- Cultivate a hobby.
- Take a "mental health day".
- Take a nap.
- Take a leave of absence.
- Eat healthier.
- Get exercise. Go for a walk.
- Enroll in a yoga, Pilates, Tai Chi, or aerobics class.
- Take up swimming, jogging, walking, rowing, or cycling.
- Get a physical checkup.
- Get enough sleep. Have a consistent bedtime and wake-up time.
- Use deep breathing, meditation techniques, and/or music to relax.
- Attitude is a choice; choose your attitude.
- Pick your battles, your hill to "die" on.
- Keep things in perspective.
- Have realistic, attainable, and measurable goals.
- Cultivate allies among students[95], staff, and parents.
- Find friends outside of teaching.
- Go to out-of-town conferences.
- Give Pat on the Backs and send thank-you notes, cards, and compliments to others. Why not send one to yourself?
- Send yourself some flowers.

- Develop positive self-talk,[96] self-control, and self-confidence.
- Cultivate a sense of humor; laugh and smile more.
- Join a professional reading group.
- Participate in a noon-hour walking club.
- Give yourself a gift of time to reflect, relax, and recharge.
- Define what success is for you, not for others.
- Believe in yourself.
- Practice random acts of kindness.
- Read motivational quotes and stories (for example, *The Last Lecture* by Pausch, R. and Zaslow, J. (Contributor).
- Collect and mount motivational posters in your classroom.
- Take a vacation, a week-end getaway, or go to a spa retreat.
- Find a significant other who can support you in good times and bad.
- Get involved with your professional teacher groups.
- Learn how to say no and set limits—you don't have to do it all. Teaching is a marathon, not a sprint.
- Limit checking your email.
- Limit your Social Media and Internet surfing.
- Unsubscribe from newsletters you don't need.
- Replace the words *can't*, *try*, and *problems* with <u>can</u>, <u>will</u>, and <u>challenges</u>.
- Be flexible or you'll be permanently bent out of shape.
- Focus on the positive.
- Join a sports league or a charitable volunteer group.
- Get a pet.
- Read a good book.
- Create a teacher portfolio of all your achievements, positive evaluation reports, uplifting notes from parents, students, teachers, and administrators. Refer to it often when you want to recharge.
- Create a vision board[97] with what you want your life to look like three, six, or twelve months from now.
- Stick to your values, your beliefs.

- Do your best, but don't be perfect. Perfection is the enemy of excellence. There is a very wide range of acceptable, yet valuable work. "Perfect" teachers are a burden to everyone, even themselves.

If your stress persists, seek professional help from your family doctor, therapist, or counsellor.

You may also want to look at a complete break from teaching. This may be starting another career, starting your own business, going back to school, or early retirement. Many people have been happier for doing so.

Consider the results from these two studies.[98] One study involved interviewing people who were dying and asking them what advice they would give their younger selves. Another major research project involved more than two hundred high-potential leaders from one hundred and twenty companies around the world. A simple question was asked to two of the brightest future leaders from each company. These were people who could command any job and salary they wanted from other companies. The question asked was, "If you stay in this company, why are you going to stay?" Here are the top three answers:

"I am finding meaning and happiness now. The work is exciting and I love what I am doing."

"I like the people. They are my friends. This feels like a team. It feels like a family. I could make more money working with other people, but I don't want to leave the people here."

"I can follow my dreams. This organization is giving me a chance to do what I really want to do in life."

These answers were exactly the same as the answers from the people who were dying. To be happy[99] in your life, you need to appreciate what you have now, and you need to maintain relationships with friends and family.

NEXT STEPS:

1. Review what is causing your stress. Focus on what you can control and ask yourself if this battle is worth fighting.

2. Keep a file of positive notes, letters, and Pats on the Back from your students, parents, and staff. Refer to them often.

3. Appreciate what you have now and maintain relationships with friends and family.

Chapter 4:

Capping your Successful Foundation

End of the Year Activities

"Education is not the filling of a pail, but the lighting of a fire."

William Butler Yeats

"If you are planning for a year, sow rice;
if you are planning for a decade, plant trees;
if you are planning for a lifetime, educate people."

Chinese Proverb

The final weeks of school are often hectic and whip by in a blur: the end-of-the-year school trip has come and gone; the final assemblies and class parties are being planned; and the final standard tests have been taken.

This is a very exciting and frenzied time. However, if you don't have a plan in place for the final days, excellent learning opportunities for you and your students could be lost. Although the end is near, there is still an excellent opportunity to review and plan for next year.

In my early years of teaching, I relied on some children's TV episodes. The episodes had great interactive activities to keep my students stimulated and learning at the end of the year. Unfortunately, as wonderful as these TV episodes were, they became outdated and boring for my students.

It's a good idea to have some "evergreen" activities available for the end of the year. You can use these activities throughout the year. An "evergreen" activity is an activity that will not become outdated any time soon. It's a good idea to have a number of "evergreen" activities available for the end of the year. These activities can also be used throughout the year as well.

Here are some end-of-the-year activities you can use.

A Trip to a French-Speaking Country

Before I had my own classroom, I taught seven classes of French every day to seventh graders for three years. The following activity was a lifesaver for me in the final weeks of school. Students really enjoyed this activity. This activity can easily be modified for other languages such as English, Spanish, Arabic, etc.

A. Choose a country to visit from the list.

B. You will have four days of class time for research and writing.

C. You will be required to give a five to ten minute oral report about your trip. This can be a skit, play, newscast, PowerPoint presentation, cooking demonstration, paintings, drawings, etc.

D. You will be required to turn in a written report. In your report draw a map of your country and answer the following questions:

1. Where did you go and why?

2. What is the capital of the country? How big is the country? How many people live there?

3. How did you travel and why (by bus, plane, train, etc.)?

4. What clothes did you take with you (consider the weather and activities you will be doing there)?

5. What did you eat? Is there a national dish?

6. What did you see (museums, buildings, mountains deserts, lakes, oceans, plays, movies, etc.)?

7. What were the people like? What do people do for work? What sports do they play? What is their national sport or game?

8. Where did you stay? What towns and cities did you visit?

9. What souvenirs did you buy?

10. What did you take on your trip besides clothes?

11. Did you like the country? Why or why not?

Countries Where French Is Spoken

Algeria	Mauritania
Belgium	Mayotte
Benin	Monaco
Burkina Faso	Madagascar
Burundi	Mali
Cambodia	Martinique
Cameroon	Mauritius Morocco
Canada	New Caledonia
Central African Republic	New Hebrides
Chad	Niger
Comoros Islands	Réunion
Djibouti	Rwanda
France	Senegal
French Guiana	Seychelles
French Polynesia	St. Martin
Gabon	St. Pierre and Miquelon
Guadeloupe	Switzerland
Guinea	Tahiti
Haiti	Togo
Ivory Coast	Tunisia
Kerguelen Islands	Vietnam
Laos	Wallis and Futuna
Lebanon	Vanuatu
Luxembourg	Zaire

Family Coat of Arms

On the family coat of arms sheet, answer the following questions in each of the numbered spaces:

1. Express in a drawing the most significant event in your life from birth to age eight.
2. Express in a drawing the most significant event in your life from age eight to the present.
3. Express in a drawing your greatest success or achievement in the past year.
4. Express in a drawing your happiest moment in the past year.

157

5. If you were guaranteed success in whatever you attempted, what would you attempt? Draw a picture of your answer.

6. Express in a drawing something that you are good at.

7. In the last space, number seven, print your family's last name.

(See the *How to Succeed as an Elementary Teacher Workbook* (found here: http://thebusyeducator.com/succeednow) for reproducible and presentation rubric for the Family Coat of Arms.)

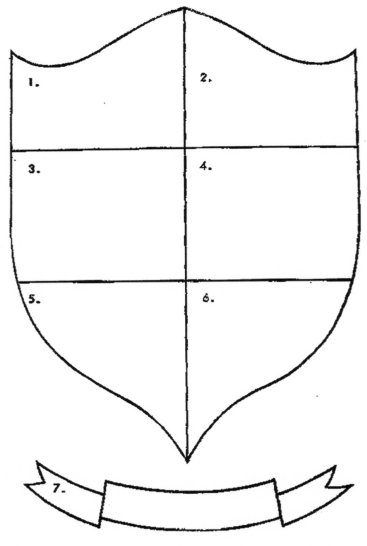

You can use the *Family Coat of Arms* activity as a stand-alone project or as an activity for the *My Autobiography* project described below:

My Autobiography

Name _____   **Date** _____

This project is about you! Begin by talking to your parents.

Your finished project should include the following:

A. A family coat of arms as a title page (see sheet for more information on how to design a family coat of arms).

B. Chapter 1 - All About Me

In this chapter, include the city and province/state where you were born; the name of the hospital you were born in; and your weight and height at birth. You may include photos, baby books, your first toy, your first shoes, etc.

C. Chapter 2 – My Family

In this chapter, you should tell us about your family. Talk to your parents about your family tree. Find out about your family name. Does it have a special meaning or significance? Is there anything in particular that your family is/was known for? How long has your family been in Canada? Do a family tree of known relatives. Grandparents will be very helpful in giving you information on your relatives. Ask them to recall stories their parents and grandparents told them about their families. Other questions you may want to ask:

- What countries do your family members come from?
- What languages do your family members speak (You may want to record some of their conversation in their own language)?
- What is one fond memory your parents have of their family when they were growing up?

D. Chapter 3 – My Friends

Who are your friends and why are they your friends? What do you like to do with them? What does friendship mean to you? Use the sheet to interview your friend (see the *How to Succeed as an Elementary Teacher Workbook (found here:* http://thebusyeducator.com/succeednow) for reproducible interview forms).

E. Chapter 4 – The Moments of My Life

What are the special or memorable moments in your life? Why? When did they happen? Was it the time you won a contest, race, or a championship?

F. Chapter 5 – Feelings, Nothing More Than Feelings

Complete the following sentences:

"To me, sad is _____."

"To me, happy is _____."

"To me, angry is _____."

"To me, to be excited is _____."

Draw a picture or include a photo of yourself showing these feelings.

G. Chapter 6 – My Like and Dislikes

Write 150 – 200 words on your likes and dislikes. What are the things that you like or dislike? What are the things people do that bother you; that make you happy?

H. Chapter 7 – My Hobbies and Interests

In this chapter, write about the things you like to do. What do you like about them? Do you enjoy sports, collecting stamps or coins, comics, reading, singing, dancing, watching movies, or playing video games? Where do you go to do these activities?

I. Chapter 8 – What Would I Do To Make The World A Better Place?

What would you change or stop to make our world a better place to live?

J. Chapter 9 – What the Future Holds for Me?

Look into the future and write what you will be doing five years from now; ten years from now; and twenty years from now. Answer the following questions: How will others describe me? What people will be important in my life? What important things will I have accomplished? What plans will I have for the future? What goals and dreams will I have? How will I be different from the way I am now?

K. The last page of your autobiography should contain a bibliography of all the sources of information you used in your project. A minimum of ten sources of information should be used.

L. Your oral presentation will be marked on the basis of creativity and originality. You may bring in some of your sources of information to show to the class.

M. You will earn extra credit for anything extra you bring to your project.

DUE DATE _____

Autobiography Checklist

Place a checkmark beside each of the activities you have completed.

1. ____ A. Family Coat of Arms Title Page completed.

2. ____ B. All About Me chapter completed.

3. ____ C. My Family chapter completed.

4. ____ D. My Friends chapter completed.

5. ____ E. The Moments of My Life chapter completed.

6. ____ F. Feelings, Nothing More Than Feelings chapter completed.

7. ____ G. My Likes and Dislikes chapter completed.

8. ____ H. My Hobbies and Interests chapter completed.

9. ____ I. What Would I Do to Make the World a Better Place chapter completed.

10. ____ J. What the Future Holds for Me chapter completed.

11. ____ K. Bibliography sheet completed.

12. ____ L. Practiced my Oral Presentation.

13. ____ M. Complete Extra Work.

Thinking about our Names

Name _____   **Date** _____

1. Do any words rhyme with your name?

   _____

2. Without unscrambling any letters, what words can you find in your first name? Middle name? Last name?

   _____

   _____

3. How many words can you make when you scramble the letters in your first name? Middle name? Last name?

   _____

   _____

4. Who were you named after?

   _____

5. Do you know your name in another language?

   _____

6. Do you have a nickname? How did you get it?

   _____

7. If you could change your name, what name would you choose? Why?

   _____

   _____

8. If the vowels in your first name were given one point and the consonants two points, what would the score for your name be?

   _____

A Research Project on Your Name

MY EXTENDED FAMILY[100]

Name _____   **Date** _____

Take six new sheets of paper.

Write your first name at the top of Page 1.

Page 2, write your middle name.

Page 3, your surname.

Page 4, your birth date and astrological sign.

Page 5, the year of your birth.

Page 6, where you were born (town, state or province, country).

PAGE 1&2 INSTRUCTIONS:

1. Find out what your name means.

2. List all the variations in the spelling of your name.

3. Find out how your name is spelled and pronounced in other languages. 'John,' for example is 'Jean' in France, 'Juan' in Spain, 'Ian' in Scotland, and 'Sean' in Ireland.

4. List five famous people who share your name and list their accomplishments.

5. List five fictional characters who share your name.

6. List five songs or poems that mention your name.

7. List five geographical locations (towns, bodies of water, countries, etc.) that share your name or variations of it.

   At home:

   Ask your parents why they chose that name for you.

PAGE 3 INSTRUCTIONS:

8. List five famous people or fictional characters who share your first and last initial. For example, if your name is Blaine Proulx, you share your initials with Brad Pitt.

9. Using your first and last initials, come up with five good two-word nicknames for yourself. For example, if your initials are A.K., you might nickname yourself 'Able Knowledge', 'Astounding Knockout', 'Apple Kutter', 'All Knowing', and 'Alien King'.

PAGE 4 INSTRUCTIONS:

1. List five famous people who share your birthday or astrological sign.

2. List five characteristics supposedly evident in people of your sign.

3. List five good things associated with the month you were born in.

4. Find out what day of the week you were born and then find out the significance or meaning of that day of the week.

5. If you were born in a hospital, who or what was that hospital named after?

At home:

If possible, get a parent to fill you in on all the relevant and seemingly irrelevant details about the day you were born.

PAGE 5 INSTRUCTIONS:

1. List five good things that happened in the world the year you were born.

2. List five popular songs of that year,

> Five popular movies,

> Five popular TV shows,

> Five inventions or discoveries,

and five world events.

PAGE 6 INSTRUCTIONS:

1. List five famous people from your town of birth, state, province, or country. What were their accomplishments?

2. List five songs or poems that mention your birthplace or country by name.

Once your research has been completed, **prepare a booklet** entitled 'My Extended Family'. Include as much as you can of what you've discovered and illustrate your booklet with photos and drawings. Illustrations could include:

– A family crest

– Your astrological sign

– Photos of famous people who share your name or initials

– Photos of singers or bands from the year you were born

– Photos of parents and grandparents

– Drawings of you enacting your new nicknames

– Photos of cities or sites that share one of your names

… and many other possibilities!

PERSONAL TIME CHART:
a One-Week Study[101]

Name _____   **Date** _____

Ever wonder where the time goes?

This chart will help you see where it goes so you can study it and make some changes if you like.

Making the chart:

On an 8-1/2 x 11 lined sheet or in a spreadsheet, write one a.m., two a.m., etc. ... twelve p.m., one p.m., etc., to the left of the margin until you have indicated a separate line for each of the twenty-four hours in a day.

Then, from the margin, draw seven lines, each ¾ **inches** apart. Above the top line, label these columns Sun., Mon., Tues., Wed., Thurs., Fri., and Sat.

This is your Personal Time Chart, on which you can log your activities over the upcoming weeks to see just when and how you're using your time.

(Note: Some activities – eating and watching TV, for example – may overlap; you may attempt to cram everything in by using abbreviations, or you may decide to do several charts, perhaps one entitled 'Things I Had to Do' and another 'Things I Chose to Do'.)

After one week: Fill in the chart with all your activities over the week and the length of time spent on each one.

Then, take several activities and calculate how much time, or what percentage of your week, you spent engaged in each activity. In calculating a percentage, you may wish to consider the whole week (168 hours) or just your awake time (168 hours minus seven nights of sleep).

Now that you know the total time, or percentage of your week, engaged in one activity, you may decide to try to decrease or increase this time by making some changes in your other activities.

The Results: Answer some of the following questions, particularly those which cause you to feel 'I'm spending too much of my life doing 'THIS'' or 'I'm not giving enough attention to 'THAT'.

How much of a week do you spend:

-sleeping?

-eating?

-at school?

-at a job?

-on the phone?

-watching TV or movies?

-listening to music?

-making music?

-in physical recreation?

-doing homework or studying?

-reading for pleasure?

-writing for pleasure?

-doing housework or grounds work?

-in religious activity?

-assisting others?

-alone?

-in a car or vehicle?

-with family members?

-with your romantic interest?

-with younger children?

-with adults?

-with animals or pets?

-doing things you like?

-doing things you don't like?

In which activities do you play an active role?

Are you getting as much out of life as you want to?

If not, what changes could you make to add pleasure and meaning to your life?

Alphabet Adventure[102]

There are 26 letters in the alphabet, and 26,000 ways to use them. Here are a few.

Grades K-8
Subjects Language Arts
Time Frame Will vary depending on the project
Materials Paper, pencils, imagination

For younger students:

- Do a shared writing chart. Pick a category and try to come up with one word for each letter of the alphabet (for example, animals, food, names, or toys).
- Sing fun alphabet songs. Some favorites are:

Backwards ABCs (to the same tune as the traditional ABC song).

Write the letters from Z to A on the board or on a chart, and point to each one as you sing. End with, "now we know our Z Y Xs, next time we will go to Texas."

I Am Learning (to the tune of London Bridge)

I am learning letter A

Letter A, letter A

I am learning letter A

a a a a a (for this line sing the sound the letter makes, not its name)

In the middle grades:

- Give one page of a newspaper to each student or pair of students. Each student should have a highlighter. Each individual or team highlights one word that starts with each letter of the alphabet on their newspaper page. This can also be done as a race.
- Challenge students to write sentences that feature words in alphabetical order. For example, "Michael never ordered pancakes". Students may pick their starting letter and work at writing longer and longer sentences.

In the upper grades

- Have students research the history of the English alphabet. Students can make a large chart showing various alphabets from around the world

(Greek, Cyrillic, Egyptian, Arabic, etc.) and use it to compare and contrast the features of each one.

- Students will write an autobiography in which each paragraph features a reflection or a facet of the student's life that begins with a given letter. For example, H for hobbies, F for family. Depending on the grade and ability level, students may be required to use all the letters or only a given number.

Book Tie-ins
There are thousands of alphabet books, from simple ABCs to wildly creative volumes. Here are some favorites:
So Many Bunnies by Rick Walton
A to Zen by Ruth Wells
Antics by Cathi Hepworth
Arlene Alda's ABC by Arlene Alda
Q is for Duck by Mary Elting and Michael Folsom
Tomorrow's Alphabet by George Shannon

Art Project[103]

In this project, students will research the life and work of an artist and recreate one of that artist's works.

Grades 1–8
Subjects Art, Language Arts, Library Skills
Materials A selection of books on art and artists from your school, public library, and the Internet; a variety of pictures of famous works of art; a supply of art materials such as paper, oil, pastels, pens, and charcoal pencils.

This project can be done successfully with many different grade levels by modifying the expectations for the written project and finished project. It was one of the all-time most successful projects in one of my schools, and most requested by teachers working with the teacher-librarian.

Brainstorm with the class the names of famous artists, paintings, sculptures, and works of art that they have heard of. Use a flow chart or mind-map to record these on chart paper (students will refer to it again at the end of the project).

On another day, do a book talk for the class with art books. Allow students to share and discuss the books over several days.

Show and display postcards or photos of selected paintings. Use postcards from art galleries, color photocopies from books, or downloaded pictures from websites. Arrange to have five or six more pictures than you have students so that each student will have a choice of several works and no one will be stuck with the last one (depending on the grade level, choose a work of art that students will later be able to reproduce without frustration). Have a group-sharing session where students share their observations and feelings about the art.

After several days observing the art, students will choose from the display a work of art that appeals to him/her. Students will then write in their journals their thoughts and feelings about that work, including how they feel while looking at it, anything they might already know about the work or the artist, what shapes and colors they see, and some words to describe the work. This journal work could be edited, rewritten, and added to the written component of the project.

The assignment is in two parts. Students will reproduce the work of art after consulting with the teacher about medium, size, and method. A hint for students when reproducing the picture is to cover the picture with clear plastic wrap or a plastic sheet and divide it into quadrants with a permanent marker. This helps them focus on each section of the work.

Students will also research the artist following the criteria/rubric established by the teacher, including country of origin, style of art, personal facts about the artist, etc. The length and format of the research project will vary depending on grade level. *Younger students* could limit their research to the name of the artist, the country he/she came from, and a couple of facts. *Upper-grade students* can format their presentation into a PowerPoint presentation.

Work together with your teacher-librarian to teach appropriate research skills, how to take notes, and how to format information.

When the art works are complete, each student will present his/her work or art to the class, along with a short summary of their research about the artist. The art should be displayed in the school, each work alongside the picture of the original. Caption the display "The New Masters". Invite other classes, school administration, and perhaps parents in to view them.

A visit to a local art gallery is a good tie-in to this project. On a visit to a major art gallery following completion of this project with a class, gallery staff were impressed with the level of knowledge the students displayed while looking at the art. Both gallery and school staff were delighted when one student bounded up to a painting, calling, "Look, it's my Picasso!"

Or you and your class can watch videos/DVDs on artists.

A related project for *upper-grade students* is to follow the same format, but instead of a work of art and artist, have each student research a famous building and architect.

> **Book Tie-ins**
> *Getting to Know the World's Greatest Artists* series by Mike Venezia.
> *Smart About Art* series (various artists).
> *Linnea in Monet's Garden* by Christina Bork and Lena Anderson.
> *I Spy: An Alphabet in Art* by Lucy Micklethwait.
> *Lulu and the Flying Babies* by Posy Simmonds.

Book Report in a Bag[104]

Teachers are always looking for ways to freshen up the traditional book report. Here is one that students enjoy.

> **Grades 4-8**
> **Subjects** Language Arts, Art, Math
> **Time Frame One or two weeks or longer.**
> **Materials** White paper bag with handles for each student; construction paper for work cards.

Students choose a book to read and report on.

Middle grade students could read a short chapter book. Be sure to have a selection of books at various reading levels and to have more books than you have students.

In upper grades, have students choose from a set of books preselected by the teacher, or allow them to choose their own. You could further refine the project by having all students choose a certain genre (for example, science fiction), or have groups of five-to-six students each working on one genre. Following their individual work, the students who worked on each genre could put together a presentation for the class outlining features of the genre, as well as a brief bibliography of the books they read.

Give each student a white paper bag with handles (approximately eight by 10 inches/twenty by twenty-five centimeters, or slightly smaller.). On one side of the bag, students will draw a cover for their book. On the other side, they will create a collage featuring various aspects of the book.

Have students measure and cut out of construction paper a number of 5-by-5 inch / 13 x 13 cm cards. (This is the math component of the project.) On these cards they will summarize various elements of the book. You will determine the number of cards according to the grade and ability level of the students.

Basic topics for cards can include the following:

1. Theme
2. Plot
3. Three Major Characters: for each character, students write the character's names, three words to describe their personality, and three words to describe their physical appearance.
4. Favorite Character.
5. Book Facts: author, number of pages, genre, publisher, and year of publication.
6. Problem / Resolution.

The cards will then be placed into the decorated bag. Students will also include a handmade artifact related to the book in their bags. For example, one student who read *Charlie and the Chocolate Factory* created a homemade chocolate bar; another student who read *Underground to Canada* linked florist wire loops together to make a chain, representing the shackles worn by slaves. Once all the material has been created, the Book Report in a Bag is handed in to the teacher.

This project works well for a variety of topics such as:

• Study of ancient Egypt (Egyptian characters).
• Native studies (totem poles).
• Novel studies (characters from the novel).
• Medieval studies (characters in period dress).

For upper grades, students can also complete a response journal entry about the book or use graphic organizers to summarize an aspect of the book. Or you can devise any other activity that suits your students, including giving them a free choice for one of the cards.

> **Book Tie-ins** *Creative Book Reports: Fun Projects with Rubrics for Fiction and Nonfictio*n by Jane Feber.

Book Talk on Video[105]

This project gives students a chance to work both in front of and behind the camera to write and deliver a compelling book talk.

> **Grades K-8**
> **Subjects** Language Arts, Drama, Media
> **Time Frame Several Weeks**
> **Materials Selection of novels or picture books; video camera.**

This project gives students a chance to study and emulate appropriate on-air skills, such as speaking slowly and clearly, using good posture, projecting personality, and being prepared. These skills are important for many other types of presentations. Students also enjoy the teamwork and the process of making and especially watching the video.

> **Book Tie-ins**
> *DK Readers: Jobs People Do — A Day in the Life of a TV Reporter* by Linda Hayward.
> *TV Reporters (Community Helpers)* by Tracey Boraas.
> *How Do I Become a TV Reporter?* by Mindi Englart.
> Reading Rainbow DVDs are available from GPN Educational Media: www.shopgpn.com

In *upper grades,* students can read a novel or a picture book and talk about the book on video using a prearranged format. In **the** *younger grades,* children can be filmed retelling a story that has been read to them.

Or to **combine activities for different grade levels,** have students from upper grades help prepare and film their younger reading buddies' book talks.

As a class, watch a video or DVD of a program such as *Reading Rainbow,* after which students do a brief book talk. Determine a format for the video presentation that will be used by the students. Post it on a chart in the classroom and, in *upper grades,* provide a copy on paper to each student, including a rubric explaining how their work will be assessed.

Do a book talk with the class to introduce them to the books you have brought into the classroom. Make sure the books you choose cover a wide range of topics. Give students access to the books. Encourage them to explore many before choosing one. Have each student choose a book that appeals to him or her.

As students read, they can make notes that will help them put together a presentation that follows the format you have already determined. Students read the book, then conference with the teacher, prepare and write their presentation, and record it on video and save.

A simple backdrop can be created in the classroom, or a school setting can be the backdrop for the on-camera reports. Depending on the grade level, students may be used to operate the camera and as directors, prompters, etc. The finished video or DVD (edited by teacher or students) can be circulated among families one night at a time for viewing.

When former students come back for a visit or run into you at the mall, it's always interesting to hear them reminisce about the things they remember and enjoyed most about their time in your class. Many students have spoken of the making and watching of these book talks as one project that was an especially fun time and a good memory.

Brown Paper Characters[106]

This project produces large 3D models that make a great classroom or school library displays.

Grades 4–8
Subjects Any
Time Frame One or two planning/instructional sessions, several sessions for painting and stuffing.
Materials A roll of brown kraft paper, paint in different colors, newspaper for stuffing.

Decide on the desired size for the finished product and cut a length of brown paper twice that size. Fold it in the middle. The front and back will be painted and stapled together, then stuffed with newspaper to create a large 3D model.

In pencil, sketch an outline of the person or figure the students want to represent on the front and back of the brown paper. When the outline is finished, paint in the outline plus any details. When the front is dry, paint the back as well.

After the back is dry, cut the figure to the desired shape and staple around three sides, leaving one of the long sides open. Carefully stuff wadded up newspaper inside, making sure the stuffing is equally distributed. Staple up the remaining side and display.

This project works well for a variety of topics such as:

- Study of ancient Egypt (Egyptian characters).
- Native studies (totem poles).
- Novel studies (characters from the novel).
- Medieval studies (characters in period dress).

Or students can make likenesses of themselves by tracing their body and following the same format for stapling and stuffing. Paint a face and hair, and dress in the student's actual clothing. This is a great project for parent interview time. When the parents enter the classroom, there appears to be someone sitting at each desk! Parents can take their brown paper son or daughter home after the interview.

Book Tie-ins
Brown Paper Teddy Bear by Catherine Allison.
What Can You Do With a Paper Bag? by Judith Cressy.
Look What You Can Make With Paper Bags by Judy Burke.

Create a Country[107]

Students can make up their own imaginary country, but they have to make it believable.

Grades 5–8
Subjects Geography, Art, Language Arts.
Time Frame Several lessons.
Materials Atlases and other research materials, paper, coloring materials.

Students will make up their own country. Their imaginary country can be placed anywhere in the world and must use information about the surrounding real countries to determine features, such as latitude/longitude, native animals, climate, and so on.

Lead-up activities to this project include a review of atlas skills and a whole-language class study of a chosen country that includes details such as:

- Name and meaning.
- Geographical location.
- Area.
- Boundaries and surrounding countries.
- Landforms.
- Climate.
- Native animals and vegetation.
- Natural resources.
- Language.
- Flag.
- Government.
- Currency.
- Time zones.

When the class study is complete, students (working individually or in small groups) will create an imaginary country, place it on a world map, and research the same categories used in the class study.

The number of details required for the assignment can vary depending on the grade and ability level of your students. They will use information about the surrounding countries to determine the features of the made-up country. The values they assign to their imaginary country must be plausible when compared with the real surrounding countries.

Each group or individual will produce a poster-sized map with notes and illustrations about their country.

Book Tie-ins
Our World: A Country by Country Guide by Millie Miller.
Any student atlas

The Mysteries of Harris Burdick[108]

The Mysteries of Harris Burdick is a mystery book composed of exquisite black and-white drawings, each with a title and a tag line, that practically beg to be written about.

Grades 4-8
Subjects Language Arts, Art
Time Frame One introductory lesson, several sessions for writing and editing
Materials A copy of The Mysteries of Harris Burdick, writing and publishing materials

Web Help
The Harris Burdick website www.themysteriesofharrisburdick.com contains teacher tips, reader's stories, an opportunity to submit stories, and a couple of animations and songs inspired by the illustrations.

In 1984, the incomparable Chris Van Allsburg published *The Mysteries of Harris Burdick*. The book's beautiful illustrations are available in a portfolio edition containing loose, oversized sheets perfect for display in the classroom.

The book begins with a letter from Chris Van Allsburg to the reader. It contains a challenge: to take inspiration from the drawings and to make up stories to accompany them. Once the students see the drawings, the lesson practically runs itself. Students may choose the drawing that intrigues them the most as the basis for their story. Follow your usual class procedure for writing, editing, and sharing.

A great follow-up to the story writing is an art lesson using charcoal pencils or sticks.

> **Book Tie-ins**
> The book tie-ins for each project are a starting point to which you will add your own choices of material to share with your students. Spend some time exploring your school library, work with your teacher-librarian, get to know a children's librarian at your public library, and be on the lookout for music, poetry, news stories, and personal experiences that you can add to what you are teaching in the classroom. Talk is essential and connections are everywhere. Your students will bring dimensions to class discussions that will amaze you. Over the course of the year, you will build a culture of shared references in discussions with your students. This will be the scaffold upon which they will stand to think, connect, create, and become lifelong learners.

Math Olympics[109]

An interactive mathematics session where students work as a team to solve problems correctly, faster than other teams.

> **Grades 3-8**
> **Subjects** Math
> **Time Frame** Ten math questions for your grade level copied and laid out in ten stations around the classroom, answer sheet, score sheet.

Write about ten math questions, including material from every strand.[110] Be sure to have logic questions, computation, and problem-solving. The questions should vary in difficulty and complexity according to grade level. Number each question. Make four or five copies of each question about the size/shape of a recipe card. Have a sheet at your desk with the answers on it that is clearly laid out for you to see, but that the runners cannot see. Also have a score sheet for each team close at hand. An 81/2-by-11-inch page separated into boxes (one per team), with the numbers one to ten in each box works well as a score sheet. Put an X through each question as the team presents you with the correct answer.

Arrange ten centers around the room. Place copies of Question One at Center One, Question Two at Center Two, and so on. Ensure that the centers are not too close together (a desk pulled off to the side of the room will function adequately).

Divide the class into teams. Try to have three to four students per team, and try to have students with a variety of ability levels working together. Number of teams will vary depending how many students you have in your class. Each team will have a designated area of the class in which to work. Have team pick *one* **runner. Only the designated runner can go get a question from a center and that same person is the only one who can come to your desk to check the answer. This cuts down on confusion and you get used to seeing the same face for a certain team.**

The teams can work at the centers in whatever order they choose. If they get a question that they can't solve, they can put it back and get another one, but each team can only work on one question at a time. If the runner comes to your desk for an answer check and has the wrong answer, the team may try again.

Students may use whatever materials they need to find the answer (toothpicks, poker chips, cubes, or any other math manipulatives you have in the classroom). A question that needs a calculator will not be a straightforward easy calculation, but more of a logic question.

Set a time limit, and the team with the most correct answers wins. It's wild and crazy and so much fun.

This activity can be interactive between classes at the same grade level. The winning team from each class or grade level can be declared and the recognized at divisional or whole-school assembly, complete with Math Olympic medals or ribbons. Teachers can coordinate the timing of this activity so that the whole school holds Math Olympics at the same time of year. Many school districts have math competitions and contests that students can be encouraged to enter based on the interest sparked by this activity.

Book Tie-ins
The Secret Life of Math **by Ann McCallum**
Math Curse by Jon Scieszka *The Grapes of Math* by Greg Tang

Play Money Spelling Bee[111]

Grades 1-8
Subjects Language Arts, Math.
Time Frame Set time limit that is appropriate for your grade level.
Materials List of easy, medium, and difficult words, class math materials, and $1, $5 and $10 bills from a game, or make your own play money designed for your class (designing the money for this activity could be an art activity culminating in a vote by the students for their favorite currency).

Prepare a list of $1 (easy), $5 (medium) and $10 (difficult) words for your grade level. Many spelling texts have all the list words in alphabetical order at the back of the book. This is a good resource to use for making the list.

Divide students into teams. Try to have four to five students on a team so they do not have to wait too long for their turn. Appoint a banker for each team to handle the money. That student holds and keeps track of the team's dollar amount.

Each student may choose the dollar level they want to try when their turn comes. Most students have a pretty good idea of their own ability level, and can choose the right level for themselves.

Explain to the students that it is better to pick a $1 word and get it right that to try a $10 word and get it wrong. Play until each student has had a turn, or the set time limit is up. The first few times you play, just run through each team once. As they get used to the game they will ask to play for a longer time.

No one is ever "out", even if they miss a word. After each turn, students go to the end of the line to await their next turn.

The team with the most money at the end of the time is the winner. Invite students to cheer each other on, but no help may be given to team members.

Book Tie-ins
The Berenstain Bears and the Big Spelling Bee
by Jan Berenstain and Mike Berenstain.

Self-Evaluation[112]

Students will fill in a blank report card form-for themselves!

Grades 3-8
Time Frame One session for set-up and explanation, one session for filling in the form, possible individual conferencing afterwards.
Materials Copies of a blank report card form.

This activity provides students with a chance to develop their self-assessment skills and teachers with an interesting insight into how their students see and evaluate themselves and their work.

A few days before report cards go home, give each student a blank copy of the actual report card they will receive. Go over it with them and explain the categories and what each one means. Have them fill in the form with the marks and comments they would give themselves. Collect the forms.

After the official report cards are sent home and students have had a chance to look at them, schedule a short interview time with each student. Discuss strengths, areas for improvement, and next steps.

Look at the student-written report card as well, and ask and answer any questions that arise. You will be surprised how accurate, insightful, and hard on themselves your students are!

Extensions

For the final report card, show students the goals they have achieved and the increase in their reading and math scores. Let them know some things they learned this year that they didn't know before.

Book Tie-ins
The Bad-News Report Card by Nancy Poydar.
The Report Card by Andrew Clements.

Stop, Drop, and Read Day[113]

This can be as big as a whole school literacy event or as small as a single-class celebration of reading.

Grades K-8
Subjects Language Arts
Time Frame Any time period up to a full day.
Materials Lots of reading materials.

This can be a whole school literacy event. Some planning by a committee or the whole staff will make this special day run smoothly. It can run for any time period, depending on how you choose to organize it. Other possibilities are a single class, grade level or division celebration of reading. A solid structure will ensure a successful event. Make a schedule for the events so you can organize appropriate time frames for each type of reading.

Ideas:

- Everyone reads from individual books quietly for one minute, mark starting and finishing points, count the words read in one minute, and come up with a total number of words for each individual and for the class as a whole (math tie-in).

- Everyone reads the same paragraph at the same time. Use a text that each student has, perhaps a page in a textbook or a photocopied page.

- Using a text that each student has, have a student read one word, then go around the whole class with each student reading one word.

- Lip reading: guess what the person is saying as they read without vocalizing.

- Share a book with a friend or group.

- Use atlases to look up place names. For example, find a place that has a girl's name, boy's name, name of a color, etc.

- Teacher reads to students.

- Choral reading: prepare a selection that you can present to another class (see page 36).

- Bring in some newspapers to share.

- Use a class set of dictionaries for "dictionary races" where students race to be the first to look up a word and read its meaning.

- Everyone reads aloud (different things) at the same time for one minute. This is silly and loud, but fun.
- Get a selection of picture books for students to read.
- Sing the words being read to the tune of the ABC song.
- Join up with a buddy class so older students can read to younger ones, and younger ones can use a book to tell a story to older ones.
- Invite special guest readers (parents, the mayor, the principal, etc.) to the school to read to students, or perhaps to read and discuss their favorite childhood book.
- Listen to an audio book (or part of one) together.
- Have a collection of materials written in other languages and students can have fun trying to figure out how to pronounce the foreign words and their meanings.
- Organize your event so that students travel from one place to another for various types of reading. For example, one class could be designated for reading newspapers, one for magazines, and one for atlas work, thus reducing the amount of materials each individual teacher must collect.
- Schedule a school-wide pizza lunch, charge the students a dollar a slice, and donate the profits to the school library or a local food bank. Parent volunteers could organize this.
- Arrange an author visit as the highlight of the day.
- Design a certificate or bookmark that can be given to students at the end of the day.

Book Tie-ins
Book! Book! Book! by Deborah Bruss.

Other end of the school activities you may want to do include math board games,[114] [115] survival scenario games,[116] and mystery units.[117] Have your students write letters of introduction to their new teacher and to students coming into your class next year.

During the last days of the school year, I made sure that the standardized tests that I gave in the first week of school and at the beginning of each term (i.e., Morrison McCall Spelling Scale, McCall Crabbs Standard Test Lessons in Reading, and Arithmetic Review) had all been done and recorded on the same class list. I did this so I could see what improvements the students had made. The list also showed me quickly and easily which students did not make any significant improvement over the year. This was the time for me to find out why. Was it my teaching? Did the students need extra help? Were there other circumstances beyond my control that account for how the students did?

To my running list of things that worked and didn't work, I could now add any observations from my standardized test results. I also took the time to organize my unit files such as math and language arts. I highlighted the difficult questions and concepts that may need extra teaching. I made these comments in my unit files and in my class teacher planner. I noted anything that needed to be fine-tuned for next year, as well as anything that worked and didn't work. I was usually doing this throughout the year, but in the rush to get things done, sometimes I forgot to note some ideas. This running list is something I'd look over during the summer. It would help me track down resources such as books, audio-visual resources, and websites to incorporate for the next year's class.

This running list was also a place to write down any moments that were especially fun with the students, and to reflect on whether they were just one-time things with this group, or whether it be duplicated with another class.[118]

During the last week, I also started collecting all the textbooks, notebooks, and leftover projects and papers. This gave me the opportunity to prepare anchor papers to show students next year. I showed students what an "A", "B", "C", "D", and an unacceptable paper look like (of course, I remove the students' names before I do this). I would also keep the notebooks and look for a record of what I did with students. Doing so gave me concrete evidence of what went well and what didn't. In some schools, notebooks are collected into student portfolios and passed on to the next teacher.

A day or two before school ended, we did a desk and class cleanup. All school textbooks and materials were returned and inventoried. Students took home their notebooks, files, projects, and personal belongings.[119] Students also checked the lost and found before the last day of school. Student lockers were cleaned. All bulletin boards were taken down, all audio-visual materials and library books were taken to the library, and borrowed items from fellow teachers were returned.

In preparation for the last day of school, I started to collect my gifts for my students. I collected books all year long to hand out the last day. Each book was unique to the student, with a personal note in the inside front cover.

The night before the last day, I placed two things in their report card envelopes. One was this poem entitled "Last Day of School", as well as a few items packed into a plastic baggie (I found this poem on the Internet many years ago. Unfortunately, I do not know its source.):

Last Day of School

You're a very special person,
And I wanted you to know,
How much I enjoyed being your teacher.
How fast the year did go!

Please come back to visit me,
As through the grades you grow,
Try hard to learn all that you can
There is so much to know!

The one thing I tried to teach you
To last your whole life through,
Is to know that you are SPECIAL
There is no one else like you!

Here are a few items to help you remember to celebrate you and your successes:
- **Toothpick** – to remind you to pick out the good qualities in others.
- **Rubber Band** – to remind you to be flexible, things might not always go the way you want, but it will work out.
- **Pencil** – to remind you to list your blessings every day.
- **Eraser** – to remind you that everyone makes mistakes, and it's O.K.
- **Chewing Gum** – to remind you to stick with it and you can accomplish anything!
- **Mint** – to remind you that you are worth a "mint".

Be sure you add:

Your Name

Grade/School/Year/City

Items for Last Day of School Survival Kit

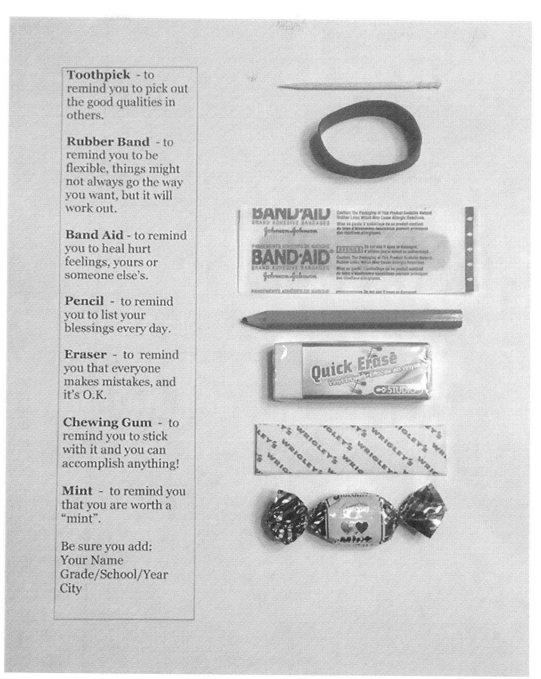

Toothpick - to remind you to pick out the good qualities in others.

Rubber Band - to remind you to be flexible, things might not always go the way you want, but it will work out.

Band Aid - to remind you to heal hurt feelings, yours or someone else's.

Pencil - to remind you to list your blessings every day.

Eraser - to remind you that everyone makes mistakes, and it's O.K.

Chewing Gum - to remind you to stick with it and you can accomplish anything!

Mint - to remind you that you are worth a "mint".

Be sure you add:
Your Name
Grade/School/Year
City

The second thing I placed in students' report cards was a list of supplies they will need for next year:

Dear Parents and Guardians,

We are looking forward to teaching your child next year. We know that you and your family are now looking forward to a great summer.

With September comes back to school shopping, and since you will want to take advantage of August sales, here is a list of supplies that will be needed bv all grade six students:

- Colored pencils
- A bottle of white glue (not glue sticks)
- A white eraser
- One each red and blue pen
- Math set
- One basic function calculator
- 12 inch/30 cm ruler
- One 1 $\frac{1}{2}$" binder (for math notes only — **do not** get a larger size)
- Two packages of loose leaf paper (one for Sept./Dec.; one for Jan./ June)
- One box of tissues
- Marker

We will be providing duotanes and notebooks. It should be noted that **there is no room in pupil desks for large hinders,** so please do not purchase any.

For safe participation in the gym program, students need proper running shoes.

Thank you for your assistance and co-operation. I wish you a safe and happy summer and look forward in meeting you in September.

This letter can be found in the
How to Succeed as an Elementary Teacher Workbook
(found here: http://thebusyeducator.com/succeednow).

As a culminating activity, I assembled for each student their autobiography. I prepared a cover sheet with their photo. I handed it out on the last day.

My

STUDENT
PHOTO

Autobiography

School
Teacher and Year

I included the following items and stapled them all together:

- Getting To Know Me questionnaire.
- Getting To Know Me Poster.
- Multiple Intelligences Survey.
- Multiple Intelligences Individual Student Profile Graph.
- Making New Friends sheet.
- My Purpose.
- Goals for the Year Parent questionnaire.
- Weekly Review Questions.
- Monthly Goal Setting sheets.
- Interview Form.
- New Year's Resolutions.
- The Metric Me.
- Family Coat of Arms.
- Year End Rapport Activity.
- Any special items (i.e. letters, photos, certificates, poems, etc.).

A week before school ended, I edited all of my videos taken over the school year. This usually resulted in a one hour video that I showed to students on the last day of school. I also invited my graduating students to come back and view their year-end video.

The last days of the school year provide an opportunity to use your students as a focus group. The same type of questions I used to "unstuck" the class, I also used in a different format to get feedback to help me in planning for next year. These questions make up my year end reflections activity:

Name _____

Year End Reflections

The miost important goal I achieved this year was...	One goal I still want to achieve is...
The best thing I learned this year was...	I enjoyed this subject the most...
The hardest challenge I had this year was...	Something I can do now that I couldn't before is...
Tliis is the name of a new friend I met this year...	Next year I will do better in...

This handout can be found in the
How to Succeed as an Elementary Teacher Workbook
(found here: http://thebusyeducator.com/succeednow).

I also did one last activity focusing on rapport. I typed all my students' names onto separate sheets of paper with three lines after each name. I photocopied and stapled the sheets, and handed one out to each student. After each name, I asked students to write down some positive words about the student. I collected the sheets. I typed up all the comments for each student onto- one sheet and cut up each of their comments. On the last day of school, I handed out an envelope with the individual and collated comments. It's a wonderful feeling for each student to get twenty-five to thirty comments about themselves that last day.

Year End Rapport Activity

Name _____

1. Anderson, Jessica _____

    _____

    _____

2. Bashir, Rema _____

    _____

    _____

3. Cirelli, John _____

    _____

    _____

...

Sample comments:

Jessica Anderson

-   You're really understanding
-   You're always smiling
-   Good skater
-   Helpful
-   Generous
-   Funny

NEXT STEPS:

1. Plan what your minimum expectations are for the last month of school.

2. Decide on teaching two to three evergreen units to your class.

3. Start preparing student portfolios for the next year's teacher or hand back to students the final day (i.e. My Autobiography).

4. Make copies of the Year End Reflection activity in the *How to Succeed as an Elementary Teacher Workbook* *(found here:* http://thebusyeducator.com/succeednow).

5. A day or two before school ends, do a desk and class cleanup. Return and inventory all school textbooks and materials. Have students take home their notebooks, files, projects, and personal belongings. Students should also check the lost and found before the last day of school. Student lockers are cleaned. All bulletin boards are taken down, all audio-visual materials and library books are taken to the library, and borrowed items from fellow teachers are returned.

6. Last Day of School Survival Kit is prepared and placed in report card envelopes.

7. Parent school supplies letter for September is prepared and placed in report card envelopes.

8. Consider teaching the Year End Rapport Activity two to three days before the last day of school.

The Last Day

"A teacher affects eternity.
He [she] can never tell where his [her] influence stops."

Henry Adams

If it's true that students only remember their first and last days of school, the last day needs to be planned and structured just as carefully and completely as the first day. This is necessary because there is so much going on that last day. Since students' (and teachers') excitement level increases as each passing hour approaches the end of the day, a structured agenda is necessary to make sure you get through all the things you want to do!

On the last day, some teachers will have a class party or schedule their class trip. Some schools will have a farewell assembly in the morning. This is to review the year and to announce the awards given to the graduating Grade Eight students the night before. There may be assemblies to introduce new teachers and to say goodbye to teachers retiring or leaving the school. There may be a community celebration in the afternoon. Often there is a party with a BBQ and music in the afternoon outside, involving parents, students, and teachers. Other schools have a teacher-versus-senior or graduating students' baseball game. Usually the last few hours of the school day are available for the teachers to say goodbye to their students.

End-of-year is a unique and precious time to ensure closure. I often told my students that it is the very last time all of us will be together as a class. some of them would move away and go to different schools, and some would be in different classes in the same school. New students and new teachers would come into the school, their classes, and their lives.

I usually started the last day as I did the first day. I met my students at the door, shook their hands, and gave them a fun activity sheet to do. Sometimes it was an activity that we didn't have time to do the very first day.

Depending on what the entire school was doing that last day, (for example, all attending an assembly), I would work around the activities with my own class. The last day was the day I brought in my video of the entire year.

This was my visual memory book. Usually the video lasted between forty-five and sixty minutes.

The highlights of the video were the time capsule presentations. I was just as amazed as the students were when they saw the changes in their physical appearance after only a year. This was a time that I would also show time capsules to my Grade Eight students. Remember I had taken them years before, when they were in my Grade Five class. Students would laugh and get embarrassed as they saw themselves and their fellow classmates.

After the video, I handed out their time capsules. Students would often spend a half hour or so reading what they wrote that particular first day. They saw how much they had grown and changed, and compared themselves to their classmates. Some teachers like to have students prepare letters to students in the previous grade telling them about what their year was like or will be. Other teachers choose to have their students write introduction letters to their next year's teacher.

Some schools hand out their yearbooks and class pictures on the last day. It's a great time for students to share memories and get autographs for their yearbooks. I told each of my students to make a record of the names of their classmates, so years from now they will remember who was in their class.[120]

I handed out birthday cards to all the students who would be celebrating a birthday during the summer holiday. We all sang a collective happy birthday to them.

I also handed out I Did It Awards for perfect attendance.

As I was about to give out the report cards, I reminded them what I told them on the first day—blink your eyes, that's how fast this year will go by.

Then I shook their hands, told them one or two quick words of encouragement, and wished them a happy and safe summer vacation. At one school I worked at, the tradition was that after the report cards were handed out, students lined the hallways. All the Grade Eights would leave their classrooms and walk down the hallways as everyone else applauded, being cheered out of their elementary schools.

What a super way to end their year and yours on the same high note on which they entered your class that very first day!

NEXT STEPS:

1. Plan and structure the last day of school just as carefully and completely as the first day.

2. Show end-of-the-year video and hand back time capsules.

3. Have students write letters of introduction to their next year's teacher.

4. Hand out birthday cards.

5. Hand out report cards.

Enjoyed This Book?
You Can Make A Difference

Thank you very much for purchasing this book *How to Succeed as an Elementary Teacher*. I'm very grateful that you chose this book from all the other wonderful books on the market.

I hope this book made your life as an elementary teacher that much more enjoyable for you and your students. If it did, please consider sharing your thoughts with your fellow teachers on Facebook, Twitter, LinkedIn and Instagram.

If you enjoyed this book and found value in reading it, please take a few minutes to post an honest review on Amazon. Reviews are very important to readers and authors – and difficult to get. Reviews don't have to be long: even a sentence or two is a huge help. Every review helps.

While on Amazon, feel free to vote for helpful reviews. The top-voted reviews are featured for display, and most likely to influence new readers. You can vote for as many reviews as you like.

Thank you for your support.

Marjan

Endnotes

1   Ginott, H. G. *Quotes*. Retrieved from https://www.goodreads.com/author/quotes/212291.

2   Some teachers prefer a class review sheet, others prefer an individual student review sheet. I have included both in the *How to Succeed as an Elementary Teacher Workbook* (found here: http://thebusyeducator.com/succeednow).

3   Morrison McCall Spelling Scale retrieved from http://www.spalding.org/images/pdf/learningathome/spellingpretest.pdf.

4   McCall-Crabbs Standard Test Lessons in Reading Retrieved from https://www.pearsonassessments.com/store/usassessments/en/Store/Professional-Assessments/Academic-Learning/DRA-Developmental-Reading-Assessment-%7C-Third-Edition/p/100001913.html.

5   The Developmental Reading Assessment (DRATM) Retrieved from

6   Chandler, C. (2017, April 9). *Beyond Learning Styles & Multiple Intelligences*. Retrieved from https://www.middleweb.com/34574/beyond-learning-styles-multiple-intelligences/.

7   *Multiple Intelligences: What Does the Research Say?* (2016, July 20). Retrieved from https://www.edutopia.org/multiple-intelligences-research.

8   Verbal-Linguistic Retrieved from http://www2.ucdsb.on.ca/t2t/Literacy%20Junior%20Capacity%20Building%20Day%201/BLM%27s%20for%20Slideshow%202/BLM%201.4.1%20Survey.doc

9   Cecil, B. *Tip #4: Be Like The Babe And Call Your Shot*. Retrieved from http://www.bestyearever.net/video/tip-4-be-like-the-babe-and-call-your-shot/.

10 Lee, R. G. *The 10 Commandments of Human Relations*. Retrieved from https://verticallivingministries.com/2012/04/24/the-10-commandments-of-human-relations-by-robert-g-lee/.

11 I celebrate birthdays by singing Happy Birthday in French and English. At the end of the French version, the whole class asks "quel age as-tu?" ("how old are you?") The student needs to say "arret" ("stop") after we reach her new age when we count the numbers in French. I give the student a birthday card with her photo and a lollipop or sucker.

12 Always inform parents and their guardians about your class activities. Get informed consent when taking photos and videos of students. The photos and videos I take are for in class use only. I do not share them outside the classroom or on social media.

13 Riley, C. (2015, August 13). *9 Weird Advantages of Being Left Handed*. Retrieved from http://www.educationandcareernews.com/learning-tools/9-weird-advantages-of-being-left-handed.

14 Lehnardt, K. (2016, September 23). *61 Interesting Facts about Left-Handedness*. Retrieved from https://www.factretriever.com/left-handedness-facts.

15   Ratledge, I. *What Your Birth Order Says About Your Personality*. Retrieved from https://www.realsimple.com/work-life/family/birth-order-traits.

16   Mcginn, D. (2017, March 18). Settling the birth-order debate once and for all. *Globe and Mail*. Retrieved from http://www.theglobeandmail.com/life/parenting/settling-the-birth-order-debate-once-and-forall-parenting/article34322380/.

17   Twins and triplets are fascinating to teach. When I was practice-teaching, I had three sets of identical twins in my class. After three weeks of teaching them, I still couldn't tell them apart!

18   One year while teaching a Grade Seven class, a student chose for his speech what it was like to be adopted. It was an emotional speech. He presented it a week after he found out he was adopted. He felt so safe with the class that he wanted to share his story.

19   Crawford, B. *Genetics for Kids*. Retrieved from http://science.lovetoknow.com/genetics-kids

20   Kindt, D. *Yarn Toss: A simple activity for demonstrating interconnectedness in language classrooms*. Retrieved from https://www.academia.edu/1418486/String_Toss_A_Simple_Activity_for_Demonstrating_Interconnectedness_in_Language_Classrooms

21   Out of the mouths of parents: this father told me, "Mr. Glavac, no matter how great a teacher you are, Jill is going to remember more of this trip than all the stuff in you class." He was right.

22   http://charlieplumb.com/ Used with permission. C. Plumb (personal email communication, Thursday, May 4, 2017 6:45 PM).

23   The pop machines have been replaced by milk and fruit juice machines. Much healthier choices!

24   *Learn to Play Chess* Retrieved from http://www.chesscorner.com/tutorial/learn.htm

25   I had a very active student. He would run up to the stage and out the gymnasium back door during physical education classes. He couldn't sit still in his desk. He would lie on the floor, shout out answers and talk to himself during silent reading. Yet, he would sit perfectly still while playing a game of chess.

26   *Why Teach Chess* Retrieved from http://chessedu.org/why-teach-chess/

27   I have used this technique with custodians. One year I had a great custodian who took a number of my students. He showed them how to wash cars. The students washed every staff car. They were happy. Staff was happy. I was happy!

28   *Ontario Today* "Cellphones in class". Interview by Rita Celli. Canadian Broadcasting Company (CBC). Air Date: Mar 14, 2017 12:00 AM ET

29   Boynton, M., Boynton, C. (2005) *Educator's Guide to Preventing and Solving Discipline Problems*. Retrieved from http://www.ascd.org/publications/books/105124/chapters/Establishing-Clearly-Defined-Parameters-of-Acceptable-Classroom-Behaviors.aspx.

30   Wong, H. K., Tripi Wong, R. (2009). The First Days of School: How to Be an Effective Teacher. Harry K. Publications, Singapore, 147–153, 157.

31   Tribes Learning Community Retrieved from https://nde.lcsd150.ab.ca/index.php/programs/tribes-process/43-tribes-for-parents-part-2/file.

32 *Painting a New Approach to Relationships.* Retrieved from http://sites.tvdsb.ca/safe-Schools.cfm?subpage=114616

33 One of my procedures was showing students how to close a door quietly. Every time a student (or staff member!) slammed my door, I had them go back and close the door quietly. I focused on this until it became a routine. One day one of my students became so upset in class that he stormed out. As he got to the door, he was about to slam it, but instead closed it quietly. All my students were amazed. As was I. Procedures do work!

34 I explain increments to students with the following examples: if they learned five new words a day times the number of school days, that's almost a thousand new words. If they learned ten new words, that's almost two thousand new words. Students' eyes just light up. It's an 'aha' moment. Here's an example I like to use to emphasize increments and the disadvantages of smoking. If you smoke one package of cigarettes a day for thirty years, you will have spent over $130,000 CDN (The price of one package of Marlboro cigarettes in Toronto Canada is C$12 at the time of writing). Two packages will cost you over a quarter of a million dollars. Those students with parents that smoke are visibly shocked.

35 Gracyk, T. 2013, June 18. *"Mother to Son" Langston Hughes poem GREAT Viola Davis voice--then POET HIMSELF RECITES!* Retrieved from https://www.youtube.com/watch?v=NX9tHuI7zVo.

36 "When people took the time to visualize exactly when and where they would do what they needed to do, they met their goals". Heath, D., Heath C. (2008 February). Make Goals Not Resolutions. *Fast Company* p. 59.

37 One of my class goals was to improve reading. To visualize student success, I posted a country map on the bulletin board. I tracked the number of pages students read each week and converted them to miles/kilometers. I plotted the class' journey on the map as a visual motivator.

38 Fellow teacher and friend Gord Harrison told me the visualization exercise he did with athletes competing in a marathon. He told them that around the 20 mile/32 km mark, they should think of someone handing them an ice cream at the end of the race. On hearing this, the athletes were skeptical, until they used it. Many reported that it gave them that much needed boost to finish the race.

39 An extension to the monthly goal activity is a weekly review sheet that students complete every week. See the *How to Succeed as an Elementary Teacher Workbook* (found here: http://thebusyeducator.com/succeednow) for a printable handout.

40 If you have room, have a *Wall of Fame* with anchor papers, letters, newspaper clippings, etc., from former students.

41 King, B. Jr. (2015, March 31). *Why Paper Planners Are Relevant in the Age of Smartphone Calendar Apps* Retrieved from http://www.makeuseof.com/tag/paper-planners-in-age-smartphone-calendar-apps/.

42 Smith, C.M. *When a Paper Planner Can Be Your Best Productivity Tool* Retrieved from http://www.lifehack.org/articles/productivity/when-a-paper-planner-can-be-your-best-productivity-tool.html.

43 Suzanne. (2013, July 15). *4 Ways To Bring Gamification of Education To Your Classroom* Retrieved from https://blog.tophat.com/4-ways-to-gamify-learning-in-your-classroom/.

44 Guido, M. (2017, February 7). *How to Gamify Learning in Your Class* Retrieved from https://www.prodigygame.com/blog/gamify-learning-in-your-class/.

45 One year I had a student struggling in my class. His strengths were outside the classroom. One day he asked me if his accomplishment of beating his dad in a series of games of darts would qualify for an I Did It Award. I was skeptical at first, until I found out how incredible his achievement was. His I Did It Award was proudly displayed with all the others. He also took home a keeper I Did It Award.

46 "No management system can be based on rewards and punishment alone," said Klementsen. "A system starts with a firm idea of what your classroom should look like when all students are actively engaged in the learning process. Then you develop a system that will help you and the students reach that goal. If the system is something that is going to take a huge amount of time and effort to keep track of, it probably won't work. If instead it is used as a catalyst to appropriate behavior, that works much better". She added, "It is more than just how they behave and how you, the teacher, react. It is how the room is arranged, how the atmosphere makes them feel, how they are seated, how the teacher greets them, when they start work, when they end work, how you get their attention, who makes the major decisions, and how those decisions are made. It's not just a bag of tricks or a bag of candy; it is a strong leader who understands his or her role as a teacher and is willing to take that leadership role and be firm and flexible at the same time". *Classroom Rewards Reap Dividends for Teachers and Students*. Retrieved from http://www.educationworld.com/a_curr/curr300.shtml.

47 *Silhouette Self Portraits* Retrieved from. https://www.kea.org/uploads/files/ScholarshipsAwards/2015/SilhouetteSelf-PortraitsLauraSchneider.pdf.

48 Bigham, L. Originally published 08/29/2005 Last updated 11/01/2006. *Drawing a Life Map* Retrieved from http://www.educationworld.com/a_tsl/archives/05-1/lesson023.shtml.

49 Life Map Images Retrieved from https://www.google.ca/search?q=Life+Map&rlz=1C-1CHZL_enCA689CA689&tbm=isch&tbo=u&source=univ&sa=X&ved=0ahUKEwi-a3Iq49uzTAhWK6YMKHdQSB4wQsAQIJg&biw=1280&bih=633.

50 I always get surprised by the variety of weekend activities students are involved in. There are the usual activities such as hockey tournaments, indoor soccer, visiting relatives, visiting friends, going to church, going to the mosque, going shopping with mom at the mall. There is always one that gives me a deeper insight into my students. One student told the class that she got on the bus all by herself (she was ten years old) to visit her dad two hours away.

51 Phonological awareness. (n.d.). *In Wikipedia* Retrieved May 16, 2017 from https://en.wikipedia.org/wiki/Phonological_awareness.

52 See *How to Succeed as an Elementary Teacher Workbook* (found here: http://thebusyeducator.com/succeednow) for a printable version of the Goals for the Year (Question #9) handout.

53 Students need to be trained for their jobs. For example, I had a script for the Door Greeter. When the Door Greeter answered the door, they followed this script: "Good Morning/Good Afternoon. Welcome to Mr. Glavac's class. How may I help you?" I told students that they only had one chance to make a good impression. This becomes a leadership lesson for them later in life.

54   Barbara Coloroso. Retrieved from http://www.kidsareworthit.com/

55   See Appendix for another version of this strategy: How to Take Control in Your Classroom and Put an End to Constant Fights and Arguments.

56   When I told students that they were in school to make mistakes, they reacted in shocked disbelief. I told them that they would learn more from their mistakes than from their successes.

57   Jon Scieszka Worldwide. Retrieved from http://www.jsworldwide.com/

58   Kids Math Long Division Retrieved from http://www.ducksters.com/kidsmath/long_division.php.

59   Examples of Mnemonics. Retrieved from http://examples.yourdictionary.com/examples-of-mnemonics.html

60   Sterling, T.V. (1994, May 29). Adapted from *Clever math wins award for teacher.* Retrieved from http://articles.baltimoresun.com/1994-05-29/news/1994149062_1_adamson-learn-math-smell-bad.

61   Canfield, J. *Visualization Techniques to Affirm Your Desired Outcomes: A Step-by-Step Guide* Retrieved from http://jackcanfield.com/blog/visualize-and-affirm-your-desired-outcomes-a-step-by-step-guide/

62   Seligman, M.E.P and Tierney, J. (2017, May 19). "We Aren't Built to Live in the Moment". *New York Times.* Retrieved from https://www.nytimes.com/2017/05/19/opinion/sunday/why-the-future-is-always-on-your-mind.html

63   Taylor, J. (2012, November 6). *The Power of Prime Sport Imagery: Athletes' Most Powerful Mental Tool Are you using mental imagery to maximize your sports performances?* Retrieved from https://www.psychologytoday.com/blog/the-power-prime/201211/sport-imagery-athletes-most-powerful-mental-tool

64   Mayberry, M. (2015, January 30). *The Extraordinary Power of Visualizing Success* Retrieved from https://www.entrepreneur.com/article/242373

65   The Troll Story. Retrieved from mrskirkcphs.weebly.com/uploads/9/3/7/7/9377405/troll_story.doc

66   *Teachers of The Secret – Jack Canfield.* Power Within Inc. 2007. DVD.

67   Lemov, D. (2010). *Teach Like A Champion: 49 Techniques That Put Students On The Path To College.* Josey-Bass, U.S.A., 207.

68   Author Unknown.

69   One year I wrapped up a queen bee container. I surprised how quickly students were able to discover what it was. Once they guessed the right answer, I brought in my bee equipment and dressed up some of my student with the bee veil, gloves and smoker. https://postalmuseum.si.edu/systemsatwork/images/global/1991_0414_1az.jpg

70   POSITIVE SELF TALK Retrieved from https://docs.education.gov.au/system/files/doc/other/area_a_personal_management_-_positive_self_talk_0.pdf.

71   http://www.chickmoorman.com/ Used with permission. C. Moorman (personal email communication, Friday, March 21, 2017 3:39 PM).

72   Moorman, C. 1993. "Rest in Peace: The "I Can't" Funeral." In: Canfield, J. and Hansen, M.V. editors. *Chicken Soup for the Soul:™ 101 Stories To Open The Heart And Rekindle The Spirit*. Health Communications, Inc. pp.156–160.

73   Canfield, J., Hansen, M.V., and Unkovich, A. (2007). *Chicken Soup for the Soul™ in the ClassroomElementary Edition: Lesson Plans and Students' Favorite Stories for Reading Comprehension, Writing Skills, Critical Thinking, Character Building*. "Rest in Peace: The "I Can't" Funeral". pp. 114–115. HCI; Elementary Ed edition.

74   McGrath, C. *No Legs, No Arms, No Worries!* Retrieved from http://ed.ted.com/on/QpfmsLex

75   Vujicic, N. "Attitude is Altitude" https://www.attitudeisaltitude.com/

76   When my two children were younger, they took karate lessons where this quote was recited the end of every session.

77   *The Wars.* (n.d.). In Wikipedia Retrieved June 4, 2017 from https://en.wikipedia.org/wiki/The_Wars. I was an extra in the movie version of this novel by Canadian Timothy Findley. The idea for this zinger came from the director, Robin Phillips. He had us do a rehearsal for a battle scene. Everything was choreographed. He gave us all instructions on where we needed to go. What he didn't tell us was that during the filming of the scene, explosions went off, a building was blown up, and horses bolted. He certainly filmed real fear for that scene, which I will never forget.

78   Bhonsle, P. (2012, August 6). *Top 10 reasons to study mathematics.* Retrieved from http://topyaps.com/top-10-reasons-to-study-mathematics

79   Tilly, M. (2016, August 6). *Why study Language Arts?* Retrieved from https://prezi.com/vmbnnmnsodzl/why-study-language-arts/?webgl=0

80   Roux, J. (2016, August 18). *Why study Civics?* Retrieved from https://prezi.com/b2cf-wkgebvqt/why-study-civics/?webgl=0

81   *Why study physical education?* Retrieved from http://seniorsecondary.tki.org.nz/Health-and-physical-education/Rationale/Why-study-physical-education

82   Alat, T. *10 reasons to study music.* Retrieved from http://gulfnews.com/news/uae/education/10-reasons-to-study-music-1.1115687

83   *10 good reasons for learning French.* Retrieved from http://www.diplomatie.gouv.fr/en/french-foreign-policy/francophony-and-the-french-language/promoting-french-around-the-world-7721/article/10-good-reasons-for-learning

84   Ibid.

85   "Contrary to popular belief, Michelangelo painted the Sistine Chapel in a standing position." Cohen, J. (2012, NOVEMBER 1, 2012). *7 Things You May Not Know About the Sistine Chapel.* Retrieved from http://www.history.com/news/7-things-you-may-not-know-about-the-sistine-chapel

86   My son was a camp counsellor and taught me these songs. These songs proved uplifting to me in a very personal way. One summer, my son and I rented a canoe in Northern Canada for a weekend of canoeing on a lake. Unfortunately, after an hour of paddling, the wind picked up and it started to rain. It seemed that the more we paddled against the wind and rain, the less distance we covered. It was also getting dark. My son started to

sing the "Toast" and "The Princess Pat" songs. The songs immediately lifted our spirits, made us focus on our paddling, and took our minds off the impending storm and night-fall. We made it to our camp site, safe and sound thanks to my son and his camp songs.

87 Lawrence, D.H. *Last Lesson of the Afternoon* Retrieved from http://www.kalliope.org/en/digt.pl?longdid=lawrence2001061512

88 Lash. R. (2004, November 5). "Want health and happiness? Be resilient". Globe and Mail. Section C. Academic, C 6.

89 Chadwick, I. "I tried to change the world and I could not. I tried to change the city where I live, and without success. Finally I tried to change my neighborhood, also without suc-cess. Until I concluded: I changed myself and my light will change others around me…". Source: The Unknown Monk Meme [Blog comment]. Retrieved from http://ianchad-wick.com/blog/the-unknown-monk-meme/109178/

90 Movie Therapy Retrieved from http://www.goodtherapy.org/learn-about-therapy/types/movie-therapy

91 My last year of teaching was very stressful. I decided to have lunch by the river every day during good weather. It helped me get through that final year.

92 Roy Halladay, All Star Pitcher. Interview by Kara Kuryllowicz. *Top of my game*. Profit October 2006. 24 "Because I have a hard time sitting down and actually going through things in my head, I have a 15 minute videotape of good pitches I've made. I play it be-fore I go to sleep the night before I pitch and at least once every five days. This gives me a reference point. It helps me develop those mental images."

93 The reference to sex, scotch, and salad is taken from Sex, Scotch, Salad Good For Heart-Doctor. It was recommended by Dr. James Key, associate professor of surgery at the University of Toronto, Toronto Canada. Retrieved from https://books.google.ca/books?id=BrwDAAAAMBAJ&pg=PA27&dq=sex+salad+and+scotch&hl=en&sa=X-&ved=0ahUKEwjukIXf7rrUAhWC7YMKHT1WDVgQ6AEIKDAA#v=onepage&q=-sex%20salad%20and%20scotch&f=false p. 27.

94 Here is a list my grade 5 students gave me before I took a one year self-funded leave of absence: Rest, go on a vacation, teach your kids, travel, visit family, meet new people, go swimming, learn karate, take dance lessons, ride a bike (make sure you wear a hel-met), hang out with friends, email friends, write a book, or help old people.

95 One year one student noticed how messy my desk was. She asked if she could organize my lessons with file folders. I said "yes!" Her mother is an administrative assistant. My student is now an elementary teacher.

96 *A simple 10 minute guide to amazing self-talk*. Retrieved from http://www.coachingpos-itiveperformance.com/simple-10-minute-guide-amazing-self-talk/

97 Rider, E. (2015, March 14). "The Reason Vision Boards Work and How to Make One". *Huffpost*. Retrieved from http://www.huffingtonpost.com/elizabeth-rider/the-scien-tific-reason-why_b_6392274.html

98 Goldsmith, M. (2004, February). "Making a Resolution that Matters". *Fast Company*, 92.

99 It's not money and possessions that make you happy. I spent four months in Guatema-la. I had a chance to visit an elementary school in Jalapa with a charitable organization

I'm involved with: Wells of Hope http://www.wellsofhope.com/. I saw presentations students were doing for parents for Mardi Gras. The school I visited had no drinking fountains, no air conditioning, no indoor washrooms. Students were happy to present in 35o C/95o F. There were no discipline problems. There were no students constantly going to the washroom. There were no complaints about the heat. Students were happily immersed in what they were doing.

100 Philips, J. (2000). Jivin' Johnny's ClassroomTeacher's EMERGENCY LessonPlans ... for elementary and high schools Over 90 student – centered lessons and projects to help YOU survive ... while your students LEARN! *MY EXTENDED FAMILY* pp. 82-85. Used with permission. J. Philips (personal email communication Fri 5/3/2013 12:19 PM). J Johnny Press 413 Mildred St., Midland ON, Canada L4R 3R7.

101 Philips. 85–86

102 Mayne, L. (Author) and Ritchie, S. (Illustrator) (2009). Great Teacher Projects: K-8. Alphabet Adventure p. 18. Boston Mills Press. Used with permission. L. Mayne (personal email communication Thu 6/22/2017 9:33 AM). https://www.amazon.com/Great-Teacher-Projects-Laura-Mayne/dp/1550465104 http://www.fireflybooks.com/index.php/catalogue/adult-books/health-beauty/product/10081-great-teacher-projects-k-8

103 Mayne, L., Ritchie, S. 22-23.

104 Mayne, L., Ritchie, S. 26.

105 Mayne, L., Ritchie, S. 28-29.

106 Mayne, L., Ritchie, S. 32-33.

107 Mayne, L., Ritchie, S. 42.

108 Mayne, L., Ritchie, S. 74-75.

109 Mayne, L., Ritchie, S. 80-81.

110 In Ontario Canada, there are five strands in mathematics. They are Number Sense and Numeration, Measurement, Geometry and Spatial Sense, Patterning and Algebra, and Data Management and Probability. Retrieved from http://www.edu.gov.on.ca/eng/curriculum/elementary/math18curr.pdf

111 Mayne, L., Ritchie, S. 87.

112 Mayne, L., Ritchie, S. 1

113 Mayne, L., Ritchie, S. 122-123.

114 Caitwalker. (2013, Oct. 13). "Create Your Own Math Board Game". Retrieved from https://www.tes.com/teaching-resource/create-your-own-math-board-game-6328487

115 Wright, Calli. " "The Big List of Board Games that Inspire Mathematical Thinking".Retrieved from https://blog.mindresearch.org/blog/big-list-mathematical-board-games

116 Survival Scenario Games. Retrieved from https://www.crystalspringsfoundation.org/docs/Survival%20Pre%20and%20Post%20visit%20activities.pdf

117 Free Mystery Lesson Plans and Units. Retrieved from http://www.mysterynet.com/learn/lessonplans/

118 Notes for next year: What was the most fun you had with your students this year? Is it duplicable with another class or was it just a one-time thing? Do you have any new experiences/adventures to (or looking to in the next year?) share with your class next year? i.e. travel, new foods, new teaching methods, art, books, films, websites, technology ,etc. How are you ensuring your legacy? Are you planting seeds and inspiring students? What fine tuning do you need to do for next year? What worked? What didn't work? Cull those files!

119 My first year of teaching, every student took a bus to the school. The last day of school, students cleaned out their desks and took all their notebooks, files, and papers on to the bus. When the bus left the school parking lot, students started throwing all their papers out the bus windows. That experience taught me to clean out their desks before the last day!

120 My father told me to do this when I was in the first grade so I wouldn't forget my classmates' names. I told my father that I would remember all their names. Years later, my father was right. I barely remember any of them.

Made in the
USA
Columbia, SC